The Civil War in London

The Civil War in London

London

Voices from the City

Robin Rowles

PEN & SWORD HISTORY

First published in Great Britain in 2018 by
PEN & SWORD HISTORY
An imprint of
Pen & Sword Books Ltd
Yorkshire - Philadelphia

ISBN 9781526706478

Typeset in INDIA by Geniies IT & Services Private Limited
Printed and bound by
CPI Group (UK) Ltd., Croydon, CR0 4YY

Pen & Sword Books Ltd incorporates the Imprints of Aviation, Atlas,
Family History, Fiction, Maritime, Military, Discovery, Politics, History,
Archaeology, Select, Wharncliffe Local History, Wharncliffe True Crime,
Military Classics, Wharncliffe Transport, Leo Cooper, The Praetorian Press,
Remember When, Seaforth Publishing and Frontline Publishing.

For a complete list of Pen & Sword titles please contact

PEN & SWORD BOOKS LTD
47 Church Street, Barnsley, South Yorkshire, S70 2AS, England
E-mail: enquiries@pen-and-sword.co.uk
Website: www.pen-and-sword.co.uk

Or
PEN AND SWORD BOOKS
1950 Lawrence Rd, Havertown, PA 19083, USA
E-mail: Uspen-and-sword@casematepublishers.com
Website: www.penandswordbooks.com

Contents

Acknowledgements

The author wishes to gratefully acknowledge the contribution of the following for their assistance and encouragement:

Alan Tucker 'AlaninBow' for his excellent photographs

Convenors and members of the British History in the 17th Century IHR Seminar Group

Curators of the Newark National Civil War Centre

Dr Anita Butler, for proofreading and improving my blurb text

Jane Young 'London Sketches' for her wonderful sketches

Members of Birkbeck Early Modern Society who kindly proofread excerpts

Members of London Historians who shared many writing tips

My dedicated guiding colleagues in Footprints of London

My editor Diane Wordsworth who did a sterling job

My fellow guides in the City of London Guide Lecturers Association

The excellent staff of the British Library

The City of London Corporation who kindly granted permission to usephotographs of Guildhall Yard

The friendly librarians of the Guildhall Library

The curators of the Museum of London civil war gallery

The helpful Institute of Historical Research library staff

The compilers of British History Online who generously allowed me to illustrate my text with quotes

The Master and Fellows of Christ's College, Cambridge for their kind permission to use the photograph of John Milton

The Master, Wardens and Assistants of the Worshipful Society of the Apothecaries of London who generously gave permission to use the photograph of Charles I 'No Smoking'

The publishing staff at Pen & Sword who were very patient and supportive throughout

Finally, to my family, friends and colleagues who have tolerated my near-obsession with the civil war years with good humour!

Introduction

As the capital of England, London by the 1640s was the largest city in the three kingdoms, with a population exceeding 500,000 people. London was the seat of power. The royal court, parliament and the Tower, with its supplies of weaponry and gunpowder, not to mention the royal mint, were all located in London. More importantly, it was the home of the City of London, the commercial hub of London to the east of the political hub at Westminster.

Geographically, the city is a square mile, a relatively small area on a modern-day map of Greater London. In an atlas of Great Britain, the city appears as a tiny dot. However, that tiny dot with its resources, money and manpower of varying allegiances was to have a significant impact on the course of the civil wars.

London, with its city livery companies overseeing professional standards of the merchants and tradesmen that populated the city. London, with over a hundred parish churches, where worshippers prayed and listened to sermons. London, where members of livery companies cut their political teeth and took social responsibility by taking their turns at civic and military offices. The city livery companies with their wealth, both financial and experiential. All these things, and more, guaranteed that London would play a driving and defining role during the civil war years.

It is important to understand the transition from Tudor England to Stuart 'Britain' before tackling the civil war years. The underlying cause of the civil wars was a delayed culture shock, exacerbated by short-term political and religious crises.

No history of the civil wars in London would be complete without an account of the London trained bands, who joined the parliamentarian armies and fought at Edgehill, Gloucester and Newbury, to name just three key battles. Finally, the later lives of some of the stakeholders, big and little, will be examined.

Note on monetary values used

To put the monetary values into context, a conservative estimate of the value of £50,000 in 1640 was approximately eight million pounds in 2016, based on calculating the increase in retail prices from 1640 to 2016. Therefore, a contribution of £3,500 is estimated to be equivalent to £572,000 nowadays. However, this method is just one of several and should be used with care, as a guideline to the probable value of the sum in question. The figures quoted throughout are the actual figures from the time.

Chapter 1

James and Charles 1603–1640

This introduction to the history of London and the civil wars of the 1640s starts at the top, with the character of the king. This is a story of a young king, intelligent and erudite, seen by many as the great hope after the disappointing last years of the previous monarch. His reign was one of reform and promised much: ecclesiastical innovation; peace in Europe; patronage of the arts; and a good working relationship with the City of London, the engine room of commerce in his kingdoms. However, this king proved to be weak in the most important aspect of his rule: politics. The young king may be compared to the rising of a new sun that promises a glorious morning, only to fade at noon, leaving an overcast afternoon, with the prospect of storms later. However, this is not an allegory of the reign of Charles I, it is that of James I.

As a prince, Charles learned from his father's example of kingship. As a king, Charles not only emulated his father, he exceeded him. Unsurprisingly, the two men were very similar in outlook. James and Charles disliked parliamentary discussion but loved philosophical and religious debates. James and Charles preferred the High Anglican form of worship. James and Charles regularly got into arguments with their respective parliaments over money. When these arguments could not be resolved, both monarchs dissolved parliament and subsisted on extra-parliamentary taxation, what nowadays may be described as 'stealth taxes'. James died in 1625 after ruling for twenty-two years, eventually broken by ill-health and disappointed in the failure of his attempted reforms. Here the comparison ends. Charles was executed in 1649 for treason against his own people, after nearly seven years of civil war. How did all of this unfold?

The year 1603 was a turning point in English history. Old Queen Elizabeth, the last Tudor monarch, now very frail and arguably politically weak in her final months, died. The question of her succession had finally been settled some years previously when Elizabeth named James Stuart, better known as James VI of Scotland, as her successor. James was the son of Mary Queen of Scots, who was executed in 1587 for plotting to overthrow her cousin Elizabeth and seize the English crown. However, Elizabeth's decision to execute her cousin

Mary almost certainly ensured that Mary's son James would be nominated to succeed Elizabeth. With a fixed succession and no rival claimant within sight, the country would at least be spared the political upheaval that took place during the Wars of the Roses in the later fifteenth century. The accession of James as king of England and Scotland was an opportunity to build on the relative stability of the Tudor era. England and Scotland had been enemies on and off since the reign of the English king, Edward I the 'Hammer of the Scots', in the late thirteenth century. Joining the two countries through the crown was a way of ensuring lasting peace. That was the theory. The actuality was that however well-planned and smoothly the handover from the Tudor to the Stuart dynasty went, the aftermath of this international merger would be far from plain sailing. In fact, the political waters of the early seventeenth century in the new country of Jacobean 'Britain' would be decidedly choppy.

The year began badly, with another outbreak of plague. Although James played the part expected of a new king and paid tribute to Elizabeth's reign, the atmosphere was uneasy. The plague epidemic in 1603 was so severe that the new king's coronation was nearly delayed and the City of London's planned pageant cancelled. The pageant was masterminded by Thomas Dekker, on the ill-chosen theme of the young king bringing a clean north wind to sweep disease out of his kingdom.[1] However, James resolved to overcome this initial setback and win over his people. James wished to unite the kingdoms of England and Scotland into a new country: Great Britain and Ireland. However, this was resisted by the English parliament in 1607 and the three kingdoms of England, Scotland and Ireland remained separate political entities, joined only through the crown that sat on James' head.[2] The notion of the three Stuart kingdoms being united into a single nation was too ahead of its time in the early seventeenth century. Although James may have been gratified to learn that political union between the three kingdoms was eventually achieved by his great granddaughter Anne, a century later in 1707, it was a long, winding and occasionally bloody process. In 1603, 'Great Britain' was a pipe dream, a Jacobean conceit.

James' first parliament sat from 1604 to 1610. There were great matters under discussion: the question of England and Scotland merging, which was voted down; and the right of the king to levy purveyance, by which goods could be purchased under the market price for use in the royal household. This was related to the Lord Treasurer's proposed, and long overdue, reform of royal finances.[3] This first Jacobean parliament sat intermittently. Sessions were adjourned for religious festivals like Easter and Whitsun, and political events such as the anniversary of James' accession, and on more serious occasions such as during the trial of the gunpowder plotters in January 1606.[4] Although the discovery and foiling of the Gunpowder Plot in 1605 temporarily boosted James' popularity, the Commons took advantage of the episode to demand that James take stricter actions against Roman Catholics. Reform of the royal finances proved to be the real stumbling block, however, and James dissolved parliament in 1611. James' second parliament, called in 1614, was nicknamed the 'addled' parliament because it achieved nothing at all during its short life.[5] Seven long years would pass before James recalled parliament in 1621.

Notwithstanding his inability to work with his parliaments, James was an active king and delighted in driving change. He helped in brokering a European peace that lasted fourteen years.[6] He commissioned a definitive version of the bible, the *King James Authorised Version*. He championed the arts and became a sponsor of the theatre: William Shakespeare's acting company, previously known as the Lord Chamberlain's Men, became The King's Men. James was an intellectual and demonstrated his breadth of interests by publishing on a variety of subjects: *Daemonologie*, a treatise on witchcraft and black magic; *The True Law of Free Monarchies*, which outlined James' theories about kings ruling by divine right; and *A Counterblast to Tobacco*, an early example of literature warning of the dangers of smoking.[7] Unlike his mother, Mary Queen of Scots, James worshipped as a Protestant. Although by about 1600 Protestantism was the settled religion in England, there were still substantial numbers of Roman Catholics secretly worshipping, according to Rome. This was illegal. However, James initially followed Elizabeth's example and practised a quiet toleration of Catholic worship. Provided they kept the king's peace and did not plot to murder him in his bed, he was content. This changed after the Gunpowder Plot. James' attitudes towards Roman Catholics hardened, just as Elizabeth's had following several Catholic-led intrigues against her person. As James cracked down on Roman Catholics, his popularity went up with English Protestants. In all matters, except one, the new king was demonstrating his credentials and his right to rule.

Right to rule was the keystone of James' political philosophy. His belief in the divine right of kings was overpowering. Despite his early popular successes, his self-belief created friction between James and his parliaments. What was happening was a delayed clash of cultures between Tudor England and Stuart Scotland. The Tudor parliaments were directed by the monarch. However, they debated issues at hand before voting. It is important to realise that parliament's function in this era was somewhat different from our modern-day parliaments. Parliament in the seventeenth century was an event, not a process, and furthermore was not a body charged with making and reforming laws for the good of the kingdom. Parliament was simply a vehicle to vote the monarch a supply of funds and then redress grievances. Over the course of the sixteenth century, in each of the parliaments called by Tudor monarchs each parliament attempted to gain purchase on the monarch by demanding 'redress before supply'. In other words, the monarch could have their funds, after grievances had been redressed. This wasn't always successful and frequently resulted in deadlock between the monarch and parliament. However, it was a very primitive nucleus of the modern parliamentary system where votes are preceded by debate.

This method of law-making was alien to James' philosophy. Scottish society tended to be clan-based and the head of each clan made the decisions. Similarly, Scots kings expected little debate in their parliaments. Scottish parliaments effectively rubber-stamped the king's requests. If James expected his English parliaments to vote on matters without an extended debate, he was going to be disappointed. Young Prince Charles and his brother Henry, coached from an early age in the art of royal governance, watched and learned their lessons well. Charles was his father's son and the old adage 'the apple doesn't fall far from the tree' was well-proven. Like James, Charles as king was a keen patron of the arts, implemented religious reforms, enjoyed exercising personal rule and disliked calling parliaments unless absolutely necessary.

The year 1612 saw the peak in James' popularity. During the previous year, 1611, James revived the old medieval rank of baronet, available to knights of good standing and easily obtainable for a fee payable to the crown. This was not unusual. There were many situations where fees were paid to the crown, such as a petition for reversal of attainder. However, James' revival of baronetcies marked a watershed between the old systems of paying dues to the crown and started the trend towards 'cash for honours'. It also marked the opening crack in the tree of governance whereby taxation was levied solely through parliament. However, in 1612, James enjoyed mixed fortunes. His long-cherished dream, seven years in the making, of producing a definitive version of the bible was realised, but this was offset with grief when his son Henry died of typhoid.[8] Overall, though, James' first decade as king of the new Britain had, despite political friction with the English parliament, gone well. Alas, a particular phrase from the Book of Proverbs in James' gleaming new bible was to be all too accurate: 'Pride goes before destruction, and a haughty spirit before a fall'.[9] Compared to his first decade on the English throne, the second half of James' reign would be near-disastrous. Prince Henry, James' first son, died of fever after swimming in the Thames. Increased friction with his English parliament made James lose all patience with the nobles and knights of the shires and in 1614 parliament was dissolved for seven years. European war, prompted by religious differences, broke out in 1618. There were further visitations of plague, and the economy slipped into 'decay of trade', or recession. The Duke of Buckingham, James' favourite at court, was everywhere. As everything that James held dear slumped, so too did his health.

In the last years of Elizabeth's reign, although never officially confirmed until the last possible minute, it was an open secret that James VI would succeed his cousin. There was a school of thought that saw James as the great hope, the young progressive monarch who would reverse and correct the failings of Elizabeth's last years. To some extent this happened and the prediction was vindicated. By the early 1620s, though, James' reign was looking like a game of two halves. The achievements of James' first decade could not offset the disappointments of the second. After the death of his elder brother, Charles was now heir to the throne and his personal qualities were starting to look kinglike. His childhood stutter and soft Scots burr never left him, but he was considered thoughtful, graceful and civil. Initially, Charles was on friendly terms with the City of London, the ancient corporation that governed the capital, supported the crown but was autonomous of royal authority. Many in the city now saw Charles as the next great hope after James. Over the course of the next fifteen years, however, the friendship between Charles and the city would be tested, strained and broken. The gleaming light of hope would gutter and fade away.

Charles' early years were also a game of two parts. Like his father, Charles' arrival as king was the chance to set the nation's ills to rights. He was his father's son and his career in the second half of the 1620s and throughout the 1630s mirrored his father's reign to an uncanny degree. Charles' first fifteen years as king were peppered with dramatic incidents that, like his father, highlighted his high intelligence, good education and his weak supply of common sense. In his last years, James had relied heavily on the advice of his favourites at court, as had his predecessor Elizabeth. In the long gaps between parliaments they told the king what he wanted to hear and he rewarded them for their loyalty. This did not necessarily make for good government. Despite his love of philosophical debate, James shied away from political debate and this could be interpreted as translating into avoiding difficult conversations. When James did make a hard decision, such as removing Edward Coke from the post of Chief Justice, this was perceived as silencing a voice of dissent rather than putting a better candidate in place.[10] Charles had grown up in the presence of favourites at court and accepted their advice to the king as part and parcel of the process of government.

Charles' political tutelage as a teenager had taken place by attending sessions in the House of Lords. In the refined atmosphere of the Upper House, Charles no doubt felt at home in the company of peers, who carried out genteel debate. It was poor preparation for dealing with the rather more rigorous cut-and-thrust of the House of Commons. Had Charles attended the Commons as often as the Lords, he might have gained an appreciation of the difference between the two houses. Parliamentary business in the Commons was necessarily urgent, dramatic and emotive. Members in the Commons had to be persuaded by rhetoric and force of argument. There was a lot of business to discuss and vote upon. When the king's business was finished, members were free to submit bills, to redress grievances, or request assistance. Many bills were presented for major or minor, even trivial, issues as Conrad Russell notes.[11] By contrast, business in the Lords was, supposedly, a calmer review of the proposed legislation, suggesting improvements. Although parliamentary business was always urgent, the pace and atmosphere of discussion in the Upper House must have seemed gentler than the bear-pit of the Commons. Charles' dislike of parliamentary debate was almost certainly a by-product of his personality. Like his father, Charles was an intellectual and a visionary, and frequently dreamt up big ideas. James' big ideas were to unite his kingdoms of England and Scotland, publish a definitive version of the bible, and broker a lasting peace across Europe. Charles' big ideas were to reform the church and improve the state of the Royal Navy. However, big thinkers are rarely able to contemplate and assimilate the maze of details that must be thought through and built up, piece by piece, to create the product of the big idea. James and Charles were intellectually far-sighted, but politically short-sighted. Their inability to focus on small details by holding regular parliaments, listening to debates and, thus, keeping in touch with the mood and concerns of their subjects, resulted in their losing sight of the overall picture.

Charles' first two parliaments, in 1625 and 1626, were disappointing. The parliament of 1625 preferred to discuss action against Roman Catholics rather than Charles' plans for joining the Thirty Years War, and was dissolved very quickly. Charles learnt from this and, before calling his second parliament in 1626, identified those members likely to oppose him and cleverly appointed them as sheriffs, thus necessitating their removal from the Commons.[12] This neat political manoeuvre might have succeeded had other issues not intruded. Charles' next disappointment came when this parliament voted him the tax rights of Tonnage and Poundage, but with strings attached. Tonnage and Poundage was charged on imports and exports. This tax was collected and paid to the king and was considered to be a perk that went with the job of wearing the crown. As this was charged by the weight and value of the goods, it was virtually impossible for merchants to evade paying the tax by manipulating the value of the goods. However, previous parliaments had voted Tonnage and Poundage to the monarch for life, whereas the parliament of 1626 only voted Charles this for one year. By effectively withholding the lifetime supply, parliament retained a degree of purchase on the monarch and hoped to force a review of royal finance and simplify the tax system.[13]

However, this parliament was swept away by its own enthusiasm for reform. Questions about Charles' support for an anti-Calvinist group in the Church of England, added to growing resentment of the role of Buckingham and now concerns about England's ability to fight in the Thirty Years War, threatened the viability of the 1626 parliamentary session.[14] At this point there was a distinct change of policy in the Commons. Whereas the 1625 parliament was anti-Catholic and relatively disinterested in the Thirty Years War, the parliament of 1626 was still anti-Catholic but rather more inclined towards a military intervention in Europe. Finally, however, by pressing for the result they wanted, the impeachment of Buckingham, the Commons brought forward their own dissolution.[15]

As an impressionable teenager, Charles had fallen under the spell of the urbane Buckingham, the most prominent of his father's favourites at court. As king, Charles did not desert his bosom friend and, until his murder in 1628, Buckingham enjoyed the rare honour of being the trusted confidante to two kings. Charles would have known of his father's difficulties in working with parliament, and having experienced two successive abortive parliaments decided to go it alone. The wars against Spain and France were financed through a Forced Loan. However, the money raised was insufficient to sustain the action and in 1628 Charles was forced to recall parliament again, his third in three years.[16] Significantly, one of the new intake of MPs (members of parliament) in the 1628 parliament was a modest gentleman farmer, Oliver Cromwell, who represented the seat of Huntingdon.[17] It's virtually certain that nobody could predict that the three kingdoms would fall into civil war, let alone that twenty-five years later a commoner would assume the role of head of state as lord protector of England, Scotland and Ireland.

There were also tensions due to the increasing influence of Queen Henrietta Maria, Charles' French and overtly Roman Catholic wife, and the presence of Capuchin Friars, who resided in the royal palace at Hampton Court.[18] On 2 March 1629, Charles lost patience and dissolved parliament in amazing and unruly circumstances. The House of Commons had attempted to pass a remonstrance against the spread of Arminianism and popery, against the payment of Tonnage and Poundage, and moved that anybody going against this would be considered an enemy of the realm and of the people.[19] The king refused to hear the remonstrance and ordered the speaker to close the parliamentary session. The assembled members protested in scenes more appropriate to a maul in a rugby match than in the Mother of Parliaments. Denzil Holles and William Strode led a party of MPs who sat on speaker of the house John Finch in an attempt to prevent him standing up to dissolve the session. The Commons then refused the king's order and sat for another two hours.[20]

Parliament was eventually dissolved a few days later, just as James had dissolved parliament fifteen years previously in 1614. However, despite the turbulent events of the 1630s, Charles maintained his personal rule for eleven years, four years longer than James managed, without calling a parliament. Stuart kings called parliaments to carry out specific business, after which they were dissolved. Parliaments that did not immediately carry out the king's will, or attempted to introduce irrelevant issues, also tended to be dissolved. If it proved impossible for business to be conducted through parliament, that business would be conducted without parliament, as James and Charles demonstrated. Meanwhile, during Charles' period of personal rule in the 1630s, events moved quickly.

In 1633, Charles appointed William Laud as Archbishop of Canterbury. Laud was a high churchman of the Arminian style of worship, of which Charles approved. Ecclesiastically, Charles and Laud were cut from the same block of wood. Charles ordered Laud to restore the lost dignity of the church, an instruction that Laud willingly complied with. Altar tables were moved from the front to the east side of the church. The tables were railed-off to emphasise their holy function and, incidentally, prevent children and dogs abusing them.[21] Dogs were constantly running in and out of churches and many parishes employed a dog-whipper, whose job it was to chase stray dogs out of the church. Laud also insisted that congregations worshipped using the *Book of Common Prayer*. This was a highly formalised, ritualised form of worship that warmed the heart of the high churchmen, but turned the stomachs of puritans, who preferred a simpler form of worship, uncluttered by stained-glass windows, and other aspects of worship resembling Catholicism. Other worshippers in the three kingdoms were also unimpressed with Laud's reforms. Presbyterian Scots, used to worshipping in their own way, resisted. Push came to shove in the bishops' wars in 1639, when Charles attempted to impose his religious reforms by military force. However, this failed when the Scots routed Charles' ill-prepared English army.[22] Had Charles a sitting parliament to vote a supply of funds for the bishops' wars, the result may have been different. This was only Charles' second visit to his homeland since his accession. In 1633, he had belatedly been crowned King of Scotland, eight years after his succession. A second English mission in 1640 ended in a negotiated peace treaty in 1641, but the message was clear: religious reform in Scotland would not be achieved by force of arms.[23]

Meanwhile, plague, that perennial unwelcome visitor, returned to London in 1630 and again in 1635.[24] The outbreak in the capital is an important factor in trying to understand the relationship between the crown and the city in the 1630s. Plague dissolved social, civic and political relationships just as effectively as the civil war would just a few years later. It was not selective in its victims, nor took any account of social class or political jurisdiction. Its only measurable effect was that by the 1630s it was more prevalent in poor, overcrowded suburbs, rather than the relatively genteel centre of London.[25] These visitations, although less severe in numbers of casualties than those of 1603 and 1625, prompted Charles to rethink how London should be organised. Charles' personal physician, Sir Theodore de Mayerne, came up with the brainwave of dividing London into five precincts, each with its own hospital.[26] This revolutionary idea could not be supported by the local political infrastructure of the day. The City of London and the Justices of Middlesex and Surrey jointly shared the responsibility for reporting and managing outbreaks of plague in London. The number of deaths and their causes in each parish were compiled by the parish clerks, recorded in the weekly Bills of Mortality, and a digest of this return was sent to the privy council. Sir Theodore's scheme with its London-wide board of health required a new political structure in London and, in 1635, the idea was put forward for a corporation of the suburbs.[27]

The corporation of the suburbs aimed to knit together those areas of London, such as the out parishes, that were part of the City of London but outside the city walls, and the liberties. These last were areas within the city's geographical limits but outside its political remit. These were a legacy from the Reformation. As Valerie Pearl notes, pre-reformation London was literally ringed with monastic houses standing in extensive grounds owned by the church.[28] After the Reformation, these lands were systematically asset-stripped during the dissolution of the monasteries in the 1530s. A century later, religious houses such as Blackfriars monastery were gone, but the liberties remained. As in the suburbs, it was possible to carry out a trade in the liberties without necessarily undergoing an apprenticeship or being subject to the regulation imposed by a livery company that was a pre-requisite of carrying out trade in the city. As Robert Ashton notes, even the acclaimed court artist Van Dyck resided at Blackfriars and, thus, was legally outside the control of the Painter-Stainers' Company.[29] Regulations regarding housing and occupancy were more loosely enforced than in the city proper, and the denizens of the liberties enjoyed the benefits of working and living under fewer restrictions. From the viewpoint of the lord mayor and aldermen, the liberties were a blot on London's civic landscape as they were parts of London that were dirty, unruly and suspected of harbouring criminals.[30] The city was aware of the risk the liberties presented, even before the Reformation, and unsuccessfully attempted to purchase them from Henry VIII.[31] However, the city was successful in eventually owning the monastic hospitals. Meanwhile, the great monastic houses and their lands had been sold off and churches converted to secular functions.[32]

It might be thought that the city would welcome the cleaning up and regulation, under its own banner, of the liberties and the suburbs. To some extent this is true. From about 1600 onwards, several schemes were hatched whereby tradesmen and producers living within 10 miles of London would be admitted to, and regulated by, the city.[33] This may have also enabled the city to quietly impose its regulation on the liberties and suburbs, as a backdoor way of absorbing them into the city proper. Although these schemes were never realised, the ideas circulating in the early 1600s confirm the city was eager to remove the anomaly of the liberties, so long as the solution benefited the city. The suburbs also presented a challenge, as businesses could flourish outside the control of the city. The obvious solution, for the city to absorb the suburbs and thus regulate their inhabitants, was, however, as Valerie Pearl notes, politically impractical. Closer political union between the city and the suburbs with their different industries might have resulted in a change in the social mix in the common council.[34] How then could the city regulate trade inside and outside the city walls without losing its own identity and social makeup? In 1608, James issued a charter to the city that attempted to tidy up all the loose ends of this problem, but the overall result was another confused mess. The city's geographical remits were extended, but the new inhabitants in the enlarged city were excused from paying local rates. They were eligible to stand for the offices of alderman, sheriff and lord mayor, and join livery companies. However, they were barred from common council and could not vote in city elections. Not surprisingly, the contradictory terms and ambiguities in this charter fuelled disputes, and the whole question of the city and the suburbs rumbled on well into the 1630s. The proposed corporation of the suburbs was, as Valerie Pearl notes, intended to solve the question of managing the expansion of London, and anomalies within its boundaries, once and for all.[35]

The city fathers, the lord mayor and aldermen, however, saw the creation of the corporation of the suburbs in 1636 as a rival, an encroachment on its special status, and in the absence of parliament, petitioned the king to register their protest:

> *Petition from the Mayor, Commonalty, and Citizens of the City of London to the King, reciting that a Patent was ready to pass the Great Seal for incorporating divers places in the city and suburbs, and three miles compass of the same, which it was thought would be very prejudicial to the liberties and privileges of the city, and praying that the Patent might be stayed, and the consideration thereof, with their reasons against it, referred to such persons as His Majesty might think fit.*[36]

Despite the protests of the city fathers, the dreaded corporation of the suburbs was created in 1636. Although they had a vested interest, the city fathers were right to be concerned. The new corporation was created by the hand of the monarch. Through the corporation's authority in the liberties and suburbs, the fingers of that royal hand penetrated into the city, possibly the thin end of the wedge towards an unknown future. There were other possibilities. The royal hand that made charters and incorporated public bodies could annul charters and dissolve corporations. The city and the corporation might be merged, in which case one of the two bodies would almost certainly be submerged, or played off against each other. Thus, the city fathers appealed to the king to reconsider. Notwithstanding its stated purpose of regulating trade and industry in the liberties and suburbs, and improving these areas of London, the corporation of the suburbs was suspected of being less of a regulatory body than a financial body. In other words, it was constructed not to encourage and enforce compliance with regulations, but through the collection of fines, to licence non-compliance.[37]

There was also a political dynamic in the city's opposition to this new corporation. During the long years of Charles' personal rule, no parliament sat. In the absence of parliament, the City of London was the largest incorporated public body in the three kingdoms. The city and the court were on friendly terms and many wealthy men were what Robert Ashton describes as concessionaires of the crown, thanks to the system of allocating monopolies.[38] Awarded by the crown, these were a crude form of market control. As Ashton notes, the issue of monopolies served many purposes. Cash-strapped royal governments could award their loyal servants monopolies and patents freely instead of making financial awards. Alternatively, monopolies could be sold, thus killing two birds with one stone. If awarded carefully, monopolies also prevented a free-for-all, with each merchant undercutting the next. On the other hand, monopolies could be unpopular. As Robert Ashton notes, the monopoly for making pins and playing cards benefitted the haberdashers, who held the monopoly, but in order to enforce the monopoly, the importation of playing cards was prohibited. This upset the importers of these goods.[39] Thus, the issue of monopolies could destabilise the market if the consequences were not thought through. Trade and commerce were regulated by the livery companies, themselves recipients of royal charters and given the right to monopolise their trade. By the 1630s, however, this system was starting to break down. Monopolies were beginning to be allocated to persons not affiliated to livery companies. Allied to the perceived attack on the city's privilege by the proposed corporation of the suburbs, in the late 1630s the city and the court were like two magnets: simultaneously drawn to and repelled from each other.

The fourth crisis was that of the extension of ship money. Charles did not share the pacific tendencies of his father. James' ideal of peace in his kingdoms effectively meant military stagnation. Charles, however, was keen to update his military forces, even though there was no standing army and barely any maritime force that could be described as a permanent navy. There was a risk that the French or Dutch fleets would dominate the seas, particularly the trading routes in the English Channel and the North Sea.[40] In times of war, ship money could be levied on the counties around the coast. Charles' innovation was to levy ship money permanently, and extend its remit to the entire country. Charles attempted this in 1628, but was forced to back down when sheriffs could not enforce payment.[41] Further writs for collection of ship money were issued and supported by the judges in 1635 and 1636. However, by 1636 it was increasingly obvious that ship money would be a permanent extra-parliamentary tax. This was resisted and challenged by MP John Hampden in the courts, who narrowly upheld the king's position that ship money was legal.[42] Legal, but only just. The judges in Hampden's trial voted seven to five in favour of the king. They may have supported the king, albeit under pressure, but to others ship money was illegal because it was a tax not sanctioned by parliament, as this petition to the king pleads:

> *We your Poor and Loyal Subjects of this your Realm of England, now grieved and oppressed with the late Taxes imposed on us, for setting out of divers Ships to guard the narrow Seas, without our Common Consent in Parliament thereunto had; do here in all Humility and Duty prostrate ourselves and this our remonstrance against the said Taxes, at Your Highness's Feet, beseeching Your Majesty of Your Royal Justice and Clemency, to take the same into Your most Just and Gracious Consideration, and thereupon to release us Your poor Subjects from this Intolerable Burthen and Grievance, under which we groan and languish, and know not how long it may continue.*[43]

The arguments about the validity of ship money continued. However unpopular the tax may have been, the main objection was it had not been passed by parliament. However, the legal challenges to ship money tend to mask one significant fact: even allowing for a degree of enforced payments, the collection rate for ship money in the late 1630s was ninety percent.[44]

To the casual student of English constitutional history, just looking at these four issues resembles a recipe for civil war: too much intervention and reform and too little consultation with stakeholders through the due process of parliamentary discussion and legislation. Yet amongst all this religious and political turmoil, ordinary life went on. The early Stuart period has been described as the high road to civil war: parliament dissolved, absolutist monarchical rule, the city and the court growling at each other like dogs. While there are elements of this, this is not the complete picture, and it is not a view echoed by the consensus of opinion of contemporary historians. What is important is that in this period, the attempted fusing of England and Scotland with their different political structures introduced stresses into society throughout the three kingdoms. All things being equal and given time, these stresses may have balanced out and tensions would be counterbalanced if not resolved. There was good reason to think this might happen. In Scotland, there were hopes of dialogue with the Scots over the prayer book. And in spring 1640, an event took place that had not been witnessed for over a decade. The king recalled the English parliament after an interval of eleven years. The big question was, after eleven years of personal rule, could the king and parliament work together?

Chapter 2

The long, the short and the fractious parliaments

The king's recall of parliament in April 1640 was not the action of a benevolent monarch wishing to exercise good governance, hear and redress his subject's grievances. The English parliament, which had not sat for eleven years following its controversial dissolution in 1629, was summoned to vote the king a supply of funds. The funds that Charles expected to be voted, without demur, were earmarked for the continuance of the Scots war, to compel usage of the *Book of Common Prayer* in the Scottish churches. The king had attempted this once before, in 1639 without success. The English army was underfunded and unenthusiastic about marching north to fight people they didn't know and probably didn't care how they worshipped. Without a parliament to vote a supply to equip the army, there was a funding gap. The king attempted to plug this by extra-parliamentary taxation, in other words, taxes levied without being agreed by parliament. This was controversial but legal. Therefore, ship money was imposed and collected, or at least requested. This still left a sizable shortfall, which the king attempted to fill with a loan from the City of London. However, this wasn't totally successful because the city only gave the king a quarter of the sum requested, £50,000 instead of £200,000.[1] Thus, the city gave the king a qualified measure of support. There are various reasons why the city did this. One explanation is that the parliamentarians-to-be, men such as Isaac Pennington, thought by loaning the king part of what he required, he would be forced to call parliament to obtain the rest. More pragmatically, the 1630s had been difficult times for trade and the city and its livery companies had felt the pinch during the decade-long recession. Although by the end of that decade there was a recovery, the livery companies still experienced some financial strain. During this time, the king confiscated the city's prize asset in Ireland, the English plantation. Although this had been restored, there was a mistrust between the king and the city, hence the city made a smaller than expected contribution.

During the 1630s, the king's business in Ireland was managed by Thomas Wentworth. In January 1633, Sir Thomas Wentworth was appointed to the position of Lord Deputy of Ireland and in 1640 was elevated to the aristocracy as Earl Strafford.[2] On 16 March 1640, the Irish parliament convened and, directed by Strafford, on 23 March, passed subsidies worth £180,000, enough to equip 9,000 men for the Scottish wars.[3] In keeping with the political practice of the Stuarts, when this Irish parliament had done its job, it was prorogued, on 31 March. Strafford, having achieved his task of raising men and money, returned to London. He persuaded the king to recall the English parliament and was confident it too could be browbeaten into voting a supply without undue delay.[4] However, the English parliament was not so compliant as its Irish counterpart. Could king and parliament work together? The short answer is no, because their objectives were contradictory.

The parliament called in that optimistic spring of 1640 later earned itself the nickname of the short parliament, because it sat for just three weeks before the king dissolved it. The short parliament achieved nothing, because it spent its time attempting to persuade the king to hear and redress grievances going back to the time just after the last parliament in 1629.[5] The king wanted his money for the Scottish war quickly and wasn't prepared to sit through speeches, debates, motions and votes for months on end. The short parliament wished to examine several key matters, all arising from the king's period of personal rule in the 1630s. When Archbishop Laud persuaded convocation to pass some half-dozen subsidies, the Commons' resisted ratifying them, standing on their traditional platform of insisting upon redress before supply. The king heard the reports of the Commons defiance while he was taking his evening meal. He abandoned his spoilt supper and summoned his enforcer Strafford, recently returned from Ireland. Strafford's advice was predictable: the king should address the Lords and persuade them to order the Commons to grant the king his supply as this was a higher priority than settling old matters.[6] The Lords in this parliament were swayed by Strafford's argument and supported the king by sixty-one votes to twenty-five. The Lords might have taken the Commons' position, however of the eighty-six peers sitting in the Lords, eighteen were bishops.[7] These were hardly likely to vote against subsidies requested by their superior, Laud. In forcing this division in the Lords, Strafford created a division within parliament having unwittingly opened a crack between the king and his supporters and the Commons. It was a bad political mistake. The Commons denounced the discussion and vote in the Lords as a breach of parliamentary privilege.[8] Memories of the previous dissolution in March 1629 must have been rekindled. Nonetheless undeterred, the Commons, led by Pym, persevered. Questions were raised about the nature and legality of the 1629 dissolution and the king's right to imprison the MPs who attempted to prevent the dissolution. Denzil Holles and William Strode had been the ringleaders in that impromptu brawl in the Commons when the speaker was restrained. Holles and Strode had been summoned to the star chamber, but refused to answer charges, maintaining their last vestige of parliamentary privilege. Holles later petitioned the king for release and, having made sureties, was released from prison in 1630. William Strode, however, refused to be bound-over and languished in prison for eleven years. He was released in early 1640 and was elected MP for the seat of Bere Alston in the short parliament.[9] Denzil Holles was elected to the seat of Dorchester.[10]

Further questions were asked relating to the king's policies during his personal rule, such as the imposition of ship money, the trial of John Hampden for refusing to pay this and the religious reforms rolled out by William Laud, Archbishop of Canterbury. These were all matters requiring debate and, where applicable, redress, before parliament would consider granting the king's supply. A model of grievances was prepared and mindful of the treatment meted out to Holles and Strode, the first priority was to secure 'Liberty of Parliament':

> *A Model of Grievances proposed, Three in Number: I. Against Liberty of Parliament. II. Against Preservation of Religion. III. Against Conservation of the common liberties of the Kingdom. These Grievances more hurtful to the King, both in point of Honour, of Profit, and of Safety, than to any other Member whatsoever, in respect of the great Interest he has in the Kingdom. Motion, that these, and such other Grievances as shall be offered here, by any Member of this House, may be first voted here; if any shall stick upon the Vote, that they may be debated; and when they are cleared, they may be, according to the ancient Customs of Parliament, presented to the Lords; and if the Lords shall allow of them, they may be presented, in a Petition from both Houses, to his Majesty.*[11]

The list of grievances offered up was endless. The Commons and king were deadlocked and even a well-meant attempt by the Lords to intercede between the two was dismissed as interference. Eventually, the king lost patience and dissolved parliament on 5 May 1640.[12] In its way, the short parliament was to Charles what the addled parliament of 1614 had been to James: short-lived, argumentative and unproductive. Unlike its predecessor in 1629, however, the short parliament was dissolved quietly and this time nobody was assaulted:

> *The Gentleman Usher of the Upper House came from his Majesty, to require the Knights, Citizens, and Burgesses, of this House, to come up presently to his Majesty: And there, by his Majesty's Command, my Lord Keeper dissolved this present Parliament.*[13]

The news of this failed parliament was dismaying in London and throughout the kingdoms.[14] The king decided to take the resources he had and press on with his Scottish war. He demanded a loan from the lord mayor and aldermen of £200,000. If this wasn't paid the king threatened to extract £300,000 from the city. On 10 May 1640, the lord mayor and aldermen voted not to support the king financially. When they appeared before the king, pointedly not bearing the list of citizens that might have made up this forced loan, four aldermen, Soames, Rainton, Gere and Atkins, were imprisoned. Strafford went so far as to warn the king he wouldn't rule in the city unless he executed the defaulting aldermen. The king threatened to force Lord Mayor Garway to relinquish the lord mayor's sword. Later, the king backed off from this, though he went through on his threat to imprison the four aldermen.[15] On 11 May, there were riots in London and at Lambeth Palace, where apprentices searched for Archbishop Laud. These were planned, not spontaneous. A few days before notices appeared in the Royal Exchange, one of the busiest parts of London, canvassing for supporters of the city, and liberty and the commonwealth, to meet on St George's Fields, Southwark.[16] They were met by the Southwark trained bands, who had been activated when news of the plot broke. The planned riot didn't take place, the trained bands occupied the fields all day. The apprentices were forced to act under the cover of darkness, but the delay was sufficient to prevent major disorder. Laud also received the warnings and had prudently closed up his house and retired to Whitehall. The apprentices' plan was thwarted again when Laud's house was ordered to be watched day and night, and the Southwark trained bands were reinforced with those of Middlesex and Surrey.[17] There were some sporadic outbreaks of disorder for a week or two. The queen was libelled and placards appeared in the city. A window at the king's palace at Whitehall was vandalised when insulting verses were etched into the glass. However, these incidents burnt out fairly quickly. The ringleaders of the Southwark riots were rounded up and executed, following a legal pronouncement that their actions were treasonable.[18]

While the short parliament had been sitting, the convocation of the Church of England was also meeting, to discuss and implement seventeen new canons devised by Laud. By convention, convocations adjourned when parliament was dissolved, but this convocation continued sitting. This was an insult to the MPs who had recently attempted to discuss grievances relating to religious innovations in the 1630s, to have further innovations imposed.[19] Meanwhile, the king's war in Scotland went from bad to worse. While the 1639 conflict ended in a stalemate and was patched up by the Pacification of Berwick, the 1640 campaign was a disaster. On 28 August 1640, the English army, commanded by Lord Conway and Sir Thomas Fairfax, was humiliated at Newburn-on-Tyne by the Scots army, commanded by Alexander Leslie. The English army was forced to retreat and the victorious Scots invaded Newcastle. This was the only pitched battle in this conflict. After this defeat, the king's war in Scotland was all but over. The war could not end without a peace treaty and the king needed parliament, to ratify this and pay off his army. In the autumn of 1640, another parliament was called. This opened on 7 November 1640 and later earned its nickname the long parliament, because it sat continually until it was forcibly dissolved by Oliver Cromwell in April 1653.

The first phase of the long parliament may be described as countering the reforms and innovations arising from Charles' period of personal rule in the 1630s. There was plenty of work to be done. The abortive bishops' wars were over and so was ecclesiastical reform in Scotland. The peace treaty required ratifying and two armies, the Scots and English, urgently needed paying off. The Scots were occupying Newcastle and each day they remained on English soil cost the Treasury £850. However, mending fences between the two kingdoms was no quick and easy repair job. It would take another year and a royal visit to Scotland before the breach of the bishops' wars even began to heal. This process was complicated by the outbreak of the Irish rebellion, the response of parliament and king to each other was hardly tactful.

What happened afterwards was quite extraordinary. On his return from Scotland, the king's progress was hailed with acclaim. In the city he was feasted and fêted, and Charles played on this to counter the opposition of John Pym and his grand remonstrance. Superficially and temporarily, and boosted by support of royalist Lord Mayor Gurney, Charles' popularity soared in London. In parliament, the grand remonstrance rumbled on. Charles' bubble of popularity in the city burst just before Christmas 1641, when the results of the city's annual elections held on 21 December saw royalists replaced with puritans. Less than three weeks later, in January 1642, Charles, fearing a parliamentary coup, made two constitutional mistakes, bad ones, when he first invaded the Commons, then Guildhall, in search of the five members (discussed below). A few days later he left London. In retrospect, it was about this time, January 1642, that parliament and the king started drifting towards civil war. The king could not dissolve parliament, thanks to John Pym's timely and far-sighted acumen in obtaining royal assent for the Triennial Act. Parliament could not be dissolved except by itself and had at least secured its own future. There would be no repeat of the unruly scenes that took place at the dissolution of the 1629 parliament, nor the unbreakable deadlock that summed up the short parliament.

Was the long parliament truly a parliament? Professor Conrad Russell has examined this question in a thought-provoking essay entitled *The Nature of a Parliament in Early Stuart England*. Professor Russell argues that the long parliament wasn't a parliament in the accepted sense and makes the following points. Firstly, the king was a member of parliament, just like the members of the House of Commons or Lords, and he sat in the House of Lords.[20] So far, so good. Professor Russell continues that parliaments were called by the king. Writs were issued for elections to the House of Commons, and the Lords were summoned to London. Therefore, a properly constituted parliament was a tripartite of king, Lords and Commons, or in other words, the king-in-parliament, advised by the Commons and supported by the Lords.[21] In January 1642, however, that structure broke. The king left London. The Houses of Commons and Lords were split. Applying Professor Russell's premise, although parliament was not dissolved in January 1642, the king's departure effectively nullified it as a parliament. Previously, the constitutional default was if parliament was sitting when the king died, parliament was automatically dissolved. But what to call it? Professor Russell points out that parliaments not summoned by the king, as happened in 1660 and 1689, were more properly conventions, or assemblies.[22] Therefore, the MPs and Lords that remained in Westminster in January 1642 were no more a parliament than the rival parliament the king had in Oxford. However, the Commons and Lords in London had no time to debate constitutional semantics. As far as they and the majority of historians agree, parliament in January 1642 was parliament. Henceforth, parliament will refer to parliament at Westminster, as opposed to the king's parliament at Oxford.

So, given the premise that parliament called in November 1640 was properly constituted, it was therefore competent to pass legislation and remained so after January 1642. Passing legislation through parliament fell into three broad phases. A bill was raised in the House of Commons, which would be debated at length and then voted upon. If the bill was rejected, it might end there, or be resurrected in a new bill later. If the bill was passed, it progressed to the House of Lords for scrutiny. If the Lords approved the bill, it was presented to the king as an Act of Parliament. The final stage was the king granting royal assent, in other words the king 'signed off' the Act into law. This is, of course, a simplification. In the context of the civil war, with the king absent and opposed to parliament, how do you create legislation into law without the authority of royal assent? The solution to this legislative impasse was the parliamentary ordinance. An ordinance was, literally, an order of parliament, a mechanism that neatly sidestepped the problem of obtaining royal assent. Once an ordinance had passed through the Commons and Lords, it was law. Parliament wasted no time. Mindful of the difficult conversation with the king, just six months earlier, when the king rejected allowing parliament to take control of the army for the relief of Ireland, the Militia Ordinance was passed on 5 March 1642:

> *The Lords and Commons in Parliament assembled have, for the Safety of His Majesty's Person, the Parliament and Kingdom, in this Time of imminent Danger, by Ordinance of the said Lords and Commons, Ordained* (here the Ordinance lists its nominations for the Militia Committee. Continues:)
> *And the said Lords and Commons have likewise Ordained, That you shall have Power to make Colonels and Captains, and other Officers, and to remove them out of their Places, and to make others, from Time to Time, as you shall think fit for that Purpose; and that you shall have Power to lead, conduct, and employ the Persons aforesaid, arrayed and weaponed, for the Suppression of all Rebellions, Insurrections, and Invasions that may happen, within the said City and Liberties thereof: and likewise shall have further Power and Authority to lead, conduct, and employ the Persons aforesaid, arrayed and weaponed, as well within the said City, as within any other Part of this Realm of England, or Dominion of Wales, for the Suppression of all Insurrections, Rebellions, and Invasions that may happen, according as you from Time to Time shall receive Directions from the said Lords and Commons assembled in Parliament.*[23]

Note the careful language used in this first parliamentary, not yet parliamentarian, ordinance. Although neither side is at war, preparations for war are taking place. The ordinance begins by clearly referencing the 'Lords and Commons in Parliament', asserting its legality. The ordinance further states its purpose is to protect the king's safety, that of parliament, and the kingdom. The ordinance is, therefore, an enabler for the common good, its only goal is the 'Suppression of Rebellions, Insurrections, and Invasions'. Finally, this short, but important ordinance concludes by gently but firmly reminding us the aforementioned committee will only be acted on upon orders from the 'Lords and Commons assembled in Parliament'.[24] The importance of this ordinance cannot be understated. Two short months after the king has, arguably, abandoned his role in the process of government, with rebellion in Ireland, parliament has acted to protect the peace of the kingdom. Professor Barry Coward has observed that the parliamentary leadership was made stronger in the aftermath of Charles' attempt to seize the five members. There was a groundswell of support for the radical atmosphere that permeated parliament in the early months of the long parliament. The demands for the removal of the king's 'evil advisors', parliamentary control over military appointments and disbarring bishops from sitting in the Upper House were popular themes that were reiterated in proposals for treaties with the king throughout the civil war.[25]

However, this first ordinance was not passed without difficulty. This is not surprising as it was a radical, no pun intended, variation from established parliamentary process. The ordinance appears to have been passed by the Commons without delay. However, the House of Lords was somewhat more cautious in dispensing with royal assent, the final stage of law-making in parliament. Petitions to parliament in January and February 1642 were accompanied by large demonstrations in London, with numbers counted in thousands rather than hundreds. A county petition against episcopal representation in parliament had between 4,000 and 5,000 supporters. Another petition from Lord Brooke, Lord Lieutenant of Warwickshire, was accompanied by hundreds of the great and the good, who rode through the city to the Royal Exchange, to this day a popular venue for demonstrations. As Professor Coward notes, behind the numbers of petitioners was an implicit threat. A demonstration in Moorfields, just outside the city, on 31 January warned of disquiet if the petition to remove the bishops was ignored. The locations for these demonstrations were well chosen, the House of Lords could hardly fail to notice. The message was taken and the Lords assented the Militia Ordinance on 15 February, although it was not finally issued until 5 March.[26]

Having passed its first piece of legislation without going through the king, parliament was more confident. At this point, ordinances were passed in the name of the king, as the *Ordinance for Raising Men for Ireland* issued on 28 May 1642 makes clear:

Whereas, by an Act made this present Session of Parliament, entitled, An Act for the speedy and effectual reducing of the Rebels in His Majesty's Kingdom of Ireland to their due Obedience to His Majesty and the Crown of England; among other Things, it is enacted, That no Part of the Money, which shall be paid in according to the said Act, shall be employed to any other Purpose than the reducing of the said Rebels, until the said Rebels shall be declared to be subdued by the said Lords and Commons as aforesaid; and that the said Money shall be employed for the speedy and effectual subduing of the said Rebels, by sending over into the said Realm of Ireland, and disposing there, such Forces of Foot and Horse, Monies, Ammunition, Victuals, and all other Things necessary to a War, in such Manner as the said Lords and Commons in Parliament shall from time to time direct; and the Overplus [surplus] of the said money, if any shall be, to be disposed as the said Lords and Commons shall likewise direct.[27]

Parliament was obviously very keen to stress that the funding earmarked for the relief of Ireland, which included the city of London's business interests in the Ulster Plantation, was ring-fenced for that purpose. There was no suggestion that the money was to be used for a war, defensive or offensive, against the king. Barely two weeks later, however, going to war with the king appeared inevitable. On 23 April 1642, the king attempted to seize the garrison, with its precious supplies of arms and gunpowder, at Hull. When he was turned away by Sir John Hotham, who later defected to the king's side, the king protested the illegality of the Militia Ordinance. The Lords and Commons replied as one, restating the validity of the Militia Ordinance and ordering officers of local authorities to execute it, promising they were protected by parliament. As Professor Austin Woolrych notes, in propagating the Militia Ordinance and their right to enforce it, parliament was stretching a rather tenuous argument that, in the absence of the king, responsibility for the well being of the kingdom and the king's person defaulted to parliament.[28] Resolving this political and legal puzzle taxed the minds of local gentry, who had to decide between complying with the ordinance or doing nothing. There was a tenuous legal precedent: the abolition in 1604 of Marian statutes regarding the militia had left the lord lieutenants in a legally precarious situation and the Militia Ordinance, as Professor Coward points out, clarified and reinforced their position.[29]

The dilemma facing the county gentry intensified in June 1642, when the king began issuing commissions of array. These were an archaic measure, a call to arms for the gentry to turn out in times of war, but had not been used for well over a century. Their legality was disputed, as was that of the Militia Ordinance. Furthermore, commissions of array reminded many of the king's period of personal rule in the 1630s.[30] The commissions were written in Latin, which was unfortunate. The English translation of the king's Latin preamble to his commission of array in *Historical Collections of Private Passages of State* begins:

> *Right Trusty, and Right Well-beloved Cousins, and Right trusty and well-beloved, we greet you well. And whereas a small Number of both Houses (after it had been rejected by the Lords in a full House, and without Our Royal Assent, or the Opinion of the Judges concerning the Legality of it) have attempted by way of ordinance, to put in Execution the Militia of the Kingdom, and to dispossess many of our ancient Nobility of the Command and Trust reposed in them by Us, and have nominated divers others who have no Interest, nor live near to some of the Counties to which they are nominated for the Lieutenancy, whereby they cannot be properly serviceable to the Counties wherewith they are entrusted; nor our People receive that Content and Security which we desire they should. To submit to the Execution of which Power by the way of ordinance, without it were reduced into a Law by Act of Parliament established by our Royal Assent, were to reduce and expose our Subjects to a mere Arbitrary Government, which by God's Grace We shall never permit.*[31]

The king opens by addressing his nobles as cousins, in other words the nobility and gentry are part of an extended family, of which the king is the head, the father of the country. Next, the king points out the legal weaknesses in parliament's justification of the Militia Ordinance, before returning to the theme that natural government resides with the 'ancient Nobility'. The king also stresses the importance of localism, that a lord lieutenant of a county knows better than those sitting in parliament. The fact that some of the nobles and county lieutenants were sitting in parliament is conveniently ignored and the Lords and Commons in parliament is dismissed as 'Arbitrary Government'. It must be admitted, however, that these are stirring words, as the king intended, and to the casual reader, the call to arms is almost irresistible. The king's use of the classical language of the Romans, however, almost certainly caused some of his subjects to make a mental connection that supporting the king was conflated with Catholicism, which was hardly the idea that the king wished to promote. The spring and summer of 1642 had seen a war of words and paper, punctuated by the occasional skirmish for control of strategic supplies, such as the standoff between the king and Sir John Hotham at Hull. However, incidents like these, although plentiful, ran counter to the national mood and the preoccupation of stakeholders on both sides wasn't how to start a war but how to avoid it. Finally, on 22 August 1642, the king lost patience. Mustering his forces at Nottingham, he raised his standard and declared war on parliament, thus forcing the difficult decision: for king or parliament?

At this point the history of parliament effectively diverges. For although part of what remained of the parliament that convened in November 1640 still sat at Westminster, another part had gone with the king to Oxford. Thus, there were two competing parliaments in the civil war. However, the London parliament had an advantage over the king's Oxford parliament: London itself. The story of the long parliament in the civil war years may be summarised thus: just over two years of inconclusive fighting that proved three things. Firstly, London, and hence parliament, the city and the Tower, was defendable and could not be taken, at least not without a massive assault by royalist forces without and assistance within. That wasn't likely to happen. Secondly, the king's army could be and was beaten. However, the third item was the sticking point. The king's army could be beaten, but not conclusively. Therefore, something had to change and that change was the Self-denying Ordinance and the creation of the New Model Army, which in little over a year systematically destroyed the king's army. This led to the inconclusive peace of 1646–47, when king and parliament struggled to find a lasting peace. Political and religious differences in parliament and its army were exploited by the king, now in custody but always thinking ahead, constantly repositioning himself in the hope of outright victory over parliament. This led to a second phase of civil war, which the parliamentarians won decisively. The long-term outcome of this would lead to Pride's Purge, the trial and execution of the king and the establishment of a republic.

Chapter 3

Heart of the city

On entering Guildhall Yard, off Gresham Street, the view is spectacular. Looking north, the fifteenth-century Guildhall was built by master mason John Croxton in the medieval Gothic style, with narrow pointed windows and ornate sculptures on the walls and roof. Behind these old stone walls stands the great hall. The flags of all the city livery companies hang here, and recorded in the stained-glass windows are the names of every mayor from Henry Fitz-Ailwin de Londonestone in 1189. In 1215, King John was forced to issue the *Magna Carta*, and one of its stipulations was the city should elect the mayor, later lord mayor, instead of accepting the king's choice – an early example of the city asserting its independence from the crown.[1]

Guildhall's magnificent fifteenth-century exterior walls are complemented by George Dance's eighteenth-century portico, in the architectural style known as Hindustani-Gothic, which skilfully merges the medieval with the age of exploration. Towering above the portico are the arms and regalia of the City of London: the shield of the City of London with its distinctive red cross of St George and the sword of St Paul. Dragons, the city's traditional guardians since about 1609, support the arms. Previous versions of the city arms had lions as supporters. The reasons behind the change are lost in the mists of time, but one school of thought believes it may reference the legend of St George and the dragon, while another thinks it possibly marks the city's autonomy from the crown, as the lion and the unicorn traditionally support the royal arms. Just above the shield sits the sword-bearer's hat, above which the city's flag flutters proudly on its flagpole. Standing to the left of Guildhall is the aldermans' court, an oddly shaped but well-loved concrete pod affectionately nicknamed 'The Pepper Pot'. Just behind this are the offices of the corporation. To the right of Guildhall stands the Guildhall Art Gallery, displaying art and artefacts from 2,000 years of London's history. These three were all built in the twentieth century.[2]

A colonnade flanks the entrance of the Guildhall Art Gallery. Inside are sculptured busts commemorating five men who left their influence on London: Richard Whittington, four times lord mayor; William Shakespeare,

England's greatest playwright; Sir Christopher Wren, who rebuilt London after the Great Fire in 1666; and Samuel Pepys, who famously recorded the fire and other notable events of the 1660s in his diary. Pepys was a cousin of Edward Montagu, the first Earl of Sandwich (not to be confused with the other Edward Montague, Earl of Manchester), a prominent parliamentarian commander during the civil wars who supported the Cromwellian protectorate in the 1650s. When this tottered in 1659, Montagu switched sides and assisted in the restoration. His reward for this service included two terms as ambassador to Portugal and Spain in the 1660s, and service in the Royal Navy during the Anglo-Dutch wars of 1665 and 1672–74.[3] Montagu was a mentor to Pepys and used his influence to assist his cousin. Their careers naturally followed similar trajectories. Although Pepys was at school during the civil war years, he supported the parliamentarians and rejoiced at the execution of Charles. At the restoration, however, Pepys joined his cousin on the royalist side and enjoyed considerable success, rising to secretary to the Admiralty Commission and elected MP for Castle Rising in 1673.[4]

Next: Oliver Cromwell, our chief of men. Cromwell is well-known as being MP for Cambridge during the civil wars, advancing from the relatively obscure rank of captain of cavalry in the Eastern Association to lieutenant-general and second-in-command of the New Model Army. Between 1648 and 1653, Cromwell sat on the council of state, then served as lord protector until his death in 1658. Just across Guildhall Yard is the church of St Lawrence Jewry, where several distant members of Cromwell's family are buried, including Doctor John Wilkins, Bishop of Chester and second husband of Cromwell's youngest sister Robina.[5] Cromwell's niece, Elizabeth, daughter of Robina by her first marriage, married John Tillotson, later Archbishop of Canterbury, at St Lawrence Jewry in 1664. Tillotson died in 1694 and was buried here.[6] St Lawrence commemorates the Christian martyr Lawrence who defied the prefect of Rome and refused to hand over the riches of the church, preferring this should benefit the poor and needy. The prefect of Rome was not impressed, and ordered Lawrence to be roasted alive on a gridiron. The visitor to St Lawrence Jewry is gently reminded of this by observing the gridiron-styled weathervane of the church.[7] The Jewry suffix reminds us this area between Gresham Street and Cheapside was the Jewish quarter of the medieval city until their expulsion by Edward I in the year 1291.[8] However, after the establishment of the Commonwealth of England in 1649, Cromwell realised that the young republic needed to establish itself as a military and financial power. To this end, Cromwell used his influence to broker the immigration of Jews from Amsterdam to London.[9] This was a difficult process, hindered externally by the first Anglo-Dutch war in the early 1650s, and by political opposition at home.[10] The Anglo-Dutch war was a regrettable complication for the young republic. Many army officers were uneasy at the thought of two Protestant nations going to war.[11] Meanwhile, in England, the debate over the readmission of the Jews continued.[12]

In the south-east corner of Guildhall Yard is a building with a green door. There is a small plaque on the wall, which is the city shield with a green hand in one of the quarters of the red cross of St George. This is the City of London's open spaces office, which manages the open spaces inside and outside the city, such as the 11,000 acres of Epping Forest in Essex.[13] Previously, this was the City of London's Irish office, which was the London connection for administering the affairs of the city's interests in Ireland. Mismanagement of affairs in Ireland was a major factor to the civil wars breaking out and, equally, a major factor in the royalists' defeat during the civil wars. Ireland, or at least the English Pale, had been run as a commercial colony since Tudor times. Periodically, and unsurprisingly, the native Irish rebelled against their English overlords. Queen Elizabeth's reign had been troubled by the problem of keeping peace in Ireland. Robert Devereux, the second Earl of Essex, overstepped his authority when he brokered a peace deal with the Irish rebels in the 1590s. Although Elizabeth forgave his disobedience, Devereux was later attainted for treason when he raised an armed rebellion against Elizabeth in 1601.[14] Although the attainder against the Devereux family was reversed under James I, Essex's divorced wife later married Somerset, one of James' favourites. This and the shame of his father's attainder may have motivated his opposition to Charles.[15]

Thomas Wentworth, later Earl Strafford, was Charles' Lord Deputy of Ireland. In the 1630s, Strafford was as ruthless in enforcing his policies, known as 'the Thorough' as Laud was in driving religious reforms. In fixing problems, Strafford made enemies. In 1628, Strafford spoke against the king and supported the *Petition of Right*, which protested against and restrained the king's right to arbitrary taxation and imprisonment, a sort of miniature *Magna Carta* for the seventeenth century.[16] Immediately this was granted, however, Strafford became the king's ally and attempted to introduce a replacement bill with watered-down terms. By the late 1620s, two broad coalitions developed. The court party supported the policies of the king, and the country party sought to restrain royal powers and clean up what they perceived as the excesses of the Caroline Court. In becoming the king's supporter, it is possible that he was attempting to steer a middle course, offering the king constructive criticism and moderating the demands made on either side. If so, he failed. In the politics of seventeenth-century England, you were expected to run with either the hare or the hounds. However, Strafford soon bounced back and, boosted by the death of the king's favourite Buckingham in 1628, was made privy councillor in 1629 and Lord Deputy of Ireland in 1632, a position he held until his recall in 1640.[17] Ireland was Strafford's downfall. In making ill-advised comments debating a pre-emptive war against Scotland, Strafford was accused of planning to use the king's Irish army to reduce England. He was impeached and tried for uttering treasonable words, but the trial was a farce and he was acquitted. However, his enemies in parliament were relentless and finally convicted Strafford by passing an Act of Attainder. Yet Charles hesitated and only reluctantly signed Strafford's death warrant. On 12 May 1641, Strafford was executed on Tower Hill, watched by thousands of spectators.[18]

The removal of Strafford merely fuelled the smouldering opposition to the court. Earl Essex famously remarked: 'Stone dead hath no fellow.'[19] Moreover, this infighting in the English political arena encouraged the Irish to rise up in October 1641. When parliament, prompted by the city, raised an ordinance to take control of the army, the king resisted.[20] This was a new departure because kings traditionally led armies into battle. The king's agreeable behaviour towards the city in November 1641, which included returning the city's estates he had previously confiscated in Londonderry, was not enough to erase the memory of this snub. The landslide results in the city elections in December 1641 show the relationship between the court and city had foundered and the mutual promises of redress and goodwill the previous November was just papering over the cracks.

Several major events took place that threatened this somewhat rose-tinted viewpoint. The first, the history of well-meant but ultimately ill-judged, corporation of the suburbs has already been discussed. The second was the bungled relief of Ireland, specifically the City of London's prized assets within the English Pale. These two incidents were dramatic enough to make the impartial observer question the strength of the long-term relationship between the city and the crown. However, during the king's triumphant return from Scotland, Charles was feasted and fêted and, as Robert Ashton notes, there was an atmosphere of reconciliation between the city and the crown.[21] Yet the damage had been done and, in city elections on 21 December 1641, the king's supporters in Guildhall were voted out of office. What had gone wrong? The answer lies in the king's treatment of the city's interests in Ireland, apparently preferring to sacrifice influence in one kingdom to focus efforts in another. The city's acclamation of the king's return was almost certainly tinged with relief that the issues in Ireland would now be addressed. Now the king had resolved, or at least stabilised, matters in Scotland, relief could be sent to the English Pale. What happened barely two weeks later, however, very nearly put the king beyond the pale.

Acting on intelligence received, Charles planned to arrest five members of parliament in January 1642 suspected of plotting with the Scots against him. The king had grievances against each of the five: John Hampden had been convicted of refusing to pay ship money in 1637, albeit by the slimmest possible majority from the panel of judges of seven votes to five. Denzil Holles and William Strode had restrained the speaker when Charles abruptly dissolved parliament in 1629. William Strode was also an enemy of William Laud, the Archbishop of Canterbury, whose high church policies veered dangerously close to Roman Catholicism in the eyes of puritans. John Pym was the loudest critic of Charles' policies, and Arthur Haselrig had less than reverential ideas about royal prerogative. Edward Montague, better known as the Earl of Manchester, was also earmarked for arrest. And there was a personal stake. It was rumoured that these men planned to indict Queen Henrietta Maria on charges of promoting Roman Catholicism, undermining the true Protestant religion of England.[22]

The king's plan discovered, thanks to a friendly warning, the six men escaped by boat into the city.[23] In the Commons, Charles demanded the men be given up, but was pointedly rebuffed by the speaker, William Lenthall, who advised the king: 'I have neither eyes to see, nor tongue to speak but as this house directs me, whose servant I am here.'[24] Lenthall obliquely referred to the Triennial Act of 1641, which stated, in part, that the Commons was independent of the monarchy and that all parliamentary business should be made through the speaker:

And likewise that the said Knights Citizens and Burgesses to be assembled at any Parliament by virtue of this Act shall and may from time to time at any time during such their assembly in Parliament choose and declare one of themselves to be Speaker for the said Knights Citizens and Burgesses of the House of Commons assembled in the said Parliament as they shall think fit which said Speakers and every of them as well for the said Peers as for the said House of Commons respectively shall by virtue of this Act be perfect and complete Speakers for the said Houses respectively and shall have as full and large power jurisdiction and privileges to all intents and purposes as any Speaker or Speakers of either of the said houses respectively therefore have had or enjoyed.[25]

The king made as dignified an exit as possible and left the Commons with cries of 'Privilege, privilege!' ringing in his ears. Charles' constitutional *faux-pas* is re-enacted at every modern-day state opening of parliament, when Black Rod, the monarch's messenger charged with summoning the members of the Commons to the Lords, has the door of the Commons chamber slammed shut in his face and he must knock three times to gain admittance, thus symbolising the independence of the Commons from royal control.[26]

Charles attempted to cover his disappointment with words, remarking he could not see any of the wanted men, and then withdrew.[27] Meanwhile, the gang of six, heroes or traitors, depending on your point of view, arrived safely in the city. There they sheltered for a while in the Church of St Stephen, Coleman Street, under the protection of radical preacher John Goodwin.[28] This parish was one of the hot spots of radicalism in the city during the civil war years and afterwards. Later the fugitive members presented themselves to the city fathers at Guildhall. On 5 January 1642, Charles repeated his ill-advised invasion of the Commons in the city. Striding into Guildhall, he demanded the surrender of the fugitive members. As in parliament, the men of the city stood firm and Charles was forced to retreat empty handed. His reception was somewhat warmer than at Westminster the previous day. In Guildhall, cries protesting privilege of parliament echoed with the occasional blessing for the king.[29] For the second time in twenty-four hours, Charles Stuart, King of England, Scotland and Ireland, was forced into an ignominious retreat from his subjects. Four days later, on 10 January 1642, the king left London permanently. He would not return until seven years later, as a prisoner under guard and facing charges of treason.[30] Meanwhile, from January to July, both sides engaged in preparations for a war that nobody wanted. Neither party wished to cast the first stone, yet England drifted slowly towards war against itself.

An analysis of the city's support for the parliamentarian forces during the civil wars falls into three phases. From 1642 to 1646, the period sometimes known as the first civil war, the city supported the parliamentarians. That is to say, a large minority of London's citizens supported parliament and another large minority went with the flow. Shortly after the drawn Battle of Edgehill in October 1642, the city fathers implemented precautions against a royalist attack.[31] It has been asserted that London's defences were as much to deter royalists in the city from making plots that could not be supported without an external royalist invasion.[32] Therefore, streets were chained at night, curfew was enforced and the number of constables increased and put on full alert.

London's first lord mayor during the civil war years was the openly royalist Richard Gurney. Gurney was a member of the Worshipful Company of Clothworkers and was master of the company in 1633. Gurney was Sheriff of London in 1633/34 and elected alderman twice: Bishopsgate Ward in 1634 and Dowgate Ward in 1637. Elected lord mayor in 1641, he impressed the king with his personal contribution when the city received the recently reconciled monarch. Gurney was awarded a knighthood and elevated to Sir Richard Gurney, Baronet of London, in December 1641.[33] His term as lord mayor was stormy. In March 1642, the recently appointed committee of safety ordered Gurney to call a meeting of common council. Gurney declined to do so, claiming to be unwell. But the matter was referred to the House of Commons, who ordered him to appoint a deputy.[34] In June 1642, during the uneasy drift to war, Gurney proclaimed for the king, and for this and other offences was impeached by the House of Commons. The House of Lords upheld the charges, and on 12 August 1642 gave their 'Judgement against the lord mayor':

> *The Lords, having taken the said Charges into their due Consideration, do find the said Sir Richard Gurney, Lord Mayor of the said City of London, guilty of causing the said Proclamation, for putting the Commission of Array in Execution, to be published, tending to the Disturbance of the Peace of this Kingdom, and of not suppressing the said Riots and Misdemeanors, and of not calling a common council, as he was by Order of Parliament required.*[35]

Gurney was barred from taking any future political offices in the City of London, or honours, and was imprisoned in the Tower of London where he died in 1647. However, he was still required to contribute to the parliamentarian coffers and was assessed for £1,000 in December 1642. Gurney refused to pay and his house was sequestered and sold to cover the default.[36] Gurney's replacement as lord mayor was Isaac Penington (sometimes spelt Pennington). Penington followed his father into the Worshipful Company of Fishmongers and served as prime warden in 1640 as well as developing business interests in the wine and cloth trades. At the time of his election to lord mayor, Penington was MP for the City of London. He confirmed his parliamentarian credentials by serving as colonel of the White Regiment in the London Regiments. From 1642 to 1645, Penington also served as lieutenant of the Tower of London and therefore was the gaoler to his predecessor as lord mayor. Isaac Penington later sat as a judge at the trial of the king in January 1649. This was the high point of his career. He continued to sit as MP for the city until 1653, and between 1649 and 1653 served on the council of state, the official title of which was the 'Executive Council of the Commonwealth of England' or 'Oliver Cromwell's privy council'. At the restoration, Penington was imprisoned in the Tower, where his health deteriorated, and he died of natural causes in December 1661.[37]

Penington's successor was John Wollaston, member and prime warden in 1639/40 of the Worshipful Company of Goldsmiths. Wollaston had many business and political interests. Sheriff of London in 1639, he represented three different wards as alderman: Farringdon Without, Dowgate and Billingsgate. In 1642, he became president of Bethlehem and Bridewell, and in 1649 took the presidency of Christ's Hospital.[38] Wollaston was knighted in December 1641, but he was a staunch parliamentarian, serving as a colonel in the trained bands from 1641 and commanding the Yellow Regiment in 1642. In December 1643, parliament passed an ordinance regulating eligibility to vote or stand in elections in the City of London, in which Sir John Wollaston was name-checked as being responsible for its implementation:

> *No Person to be Elected or have voice in election that hath been a malignant, or that shall not take late Solemn League and Covenant Sir J. Wollaston and others to see this Ord. executed.*[39]

Thomas Atkins had political interests in London and Norwich. An alderman of Norwich he also sat as MP for that city in 1640 and from 1647 to 1653. Atkins served as alderman for Bridge Ward Without, the northern part of modern day Southwark, and was one of the four aldermen imprisoned in the Tower in 1640 for refusing to give the king names of persons deemed able to lend £50 or more. Atkins served as colonel in the Norwich militia, but found time to serve as lord mayor in 1644. He was a republican and supporter of Oliver Cromwell. At the restoration, his political stance proved unacceptable and he was discharged from his office of alderman.[40]

The lord mayors of London from 1642 to 1645 all supported the parliamentarian cause. However, in the elections of 1645, Sir Thomas Adams, a royalist and member of the Worshipful Company of Drapers, was elected. This was surprising because Sir Thomas had been suspected of concealing the king at the outbreak of the civil war. After his house was searched Sir Thomas was committed to the Tower as a precaution. However, he proved himself to be diligent and scrupulous in his public service: he gave up his business interests, exposed a fraud being perpetrated by a steward of

St Thomas's Hospital, and reportedly refused to use his official position to enrich himself.[41] Sir Thomas was succeeded as lord mayor by John Gayer in 1646. Gayer was a fishmonger and elected prime warden of the company in 1638. From 1639 to 1642, he was colonel of the trained bands. In 1640, Gayer and fellow aldermen Nicholas Rainton, Thomas Soame and Thomas Atkins were imprisoned for failing to organise contributions to lend the king funds. However, as part of the king's rapprochement exercise with the city in late 1641, Gayer was knighted. Apart from his service in the trained bands, Gayer spent the civil war years in civic affairs, sitting on the management committee of the East India Company from 1641 to 1649, and president of Christ's Hospital in 1648.[42]

Little is known about John Warner, Gayer's successor. Warner was a grocer and served as Sheriff of London in 1639/40. He was elected as alderman for Queenhithe Ward in 1640 and served as colonel in the London Green Regiment of Foot from 1642 to 1645.[43] Warner was elected lord mayor in 1647, and his greatest contribution was keeping the peace in London. In December that year, the London apprentices rioted in favour of keeping Christmas. They dressed a pump in Cornhill in a cloak of holly and ivy and drove off the soldiers who attempted to remove the green decorations. Warner made a personal appearance and restored order.[44] Possibly because of this, Warner's house was attacked when the apprentices rioted again in April 1648.[45] In June, royalists in Kent rose up under the command of Earl Norwich. but were beaten off. Crossing the River Thames, they mustered at Stratford and Bow. Despite gaining recruits from London, Norwich was unable to enter the city. Warner, aided by Skippon, used his contacts and had the gates shut at Mile End.[46] He died in late October 1648, just days short of completing his year in office.[47]

Although in 1648, when civil war broke out again while the city remained neutral, ever louder and more urgent voices were calling for negotiations with the king. The city elected its third pro-royalist lord mayor, Abraham Reynardson, a merchant taylor. Reynardson co-operated in raising loans for the king in 1640, but resisted, until compelled, helping to raise funds for the parliamentarian cause in 1642/43.[48] After his election as lord mayor in 1648, Reynardson was troublesome for the city and parliament. He continued to require newly elected common councillors to take oaths of loyalty, ignoring parliament's directive that taking oaths was illegal. In January 1649, the recently purged parliament ordered Reynardson to reverse this policy and remove the chains recently installed to prevent cavalry patrolling the city streets. Reynardson refused to read the notice proclaiming the king's trial, which was read in his absence by the sergeant-at-arms. Reynardson also avoided holding a vote in a meeting discussing a petition that declared the House of Commons in parliament was the supreme authority of the country. Oddly, parliament did not censure him for these repeated acts of defiance, and in the eyes of royalists, he was a hero.[49] However, in March 1649, parliament lost patience. Reynardson was summoned to the Commons to defend his actions in refusing to publish the act abolishing the monarchy. Despite his plea of acting in the public interest according to his conscience, he was fined £2,000 and stripped of his mayoralty. Reynardson refused to pay. His assets were seized and auctioned to pay the fine. He served two terms on the committee of the East India Company in the 1650s, but otherwise played little part in politics. Reynardson was belatedly rewarded for his loyalty to the crown with a knighthood at the restoration. However, by then he was elderly and in poor health. He died at Tottenham in 1661.[50]

Reynardson's replacement was Sir Thomas Andrewes, who served as lord mayor from April to October 1649. Sir Thomas was a leather-seller by trade, although he diversified into international trade and finance.[51] During the war years, he was an active member of various financial committees at Guildhall, notably as treasurer of money and plate. In 1649, he sat as commissioner at the king's trial. Although not a signatory to the king's death warrant, he approved the sentence of the court and witnessed the king's execution on 30 January 1649. On 23 March that same year, he read in the city the act abolishing the office of the king, when his predecessor refused to do so. Sir Thomas's actions earned him the prized office of lord mayor. He proved himself to be parliament's man in London and was re-elected in 1650.[52]

After the king's execution, the city demonstrated its loyalty to the new regime. In June 1649, officers of the New Model Army worshipped at the church of Christchurch Greyfriars, on Newgate Street, to celebrate, as they thought, peace in the three kingdoms. Afterwards, the officers marched through the city to Grocers Hall on Princes Street, where they were feasted and fêted.[53] The choice of Christchurch Greyfriars is interesting. It was the largest church in London, being the church of the Greyfriars monastery, which became a hospital at the Reformation. In 1647, the church was home to a committee that had been established to wind-up and pay-off the New Model Army, a measure that proved to be premature.[54] However, the New Model Army wasn't going to quietly disappear. Neither was Lord Fairfax. Fairfax swallowed his misgivings about the new republic for the greater good. He remained as captain-general of the New Model Army and kept on friendly terms with his officers. There was still work to be done. The

Levellers threatened the discipline of the army. The year 1649 saw Leveller-instigated mutinies at Banbury, Burford and Bishopsgate in the city. The grandees, the senior commanders of the army, could not agree to the radical settlement the Levellers demanded. The mutinies were quelled, the ringleaders executed and the Leveller movement was crushed before it could spark another kind of civil war.[55]

During his second term as lord mayor, Sir Thomas Andrewes ensured there were no disturbances in the capital during this third phase of the civil war in 1649–51. Sir Thomas sat on the committee of the East India Company in the 1650s and was knighted by Oliver Cromwell in 1657. He died in August 1659 and was spared the decision of fleeing or being tried for his life as a regicide at the restoration. However, the Indemnity and Oblivion Act 1660 did not protect him and his estates and property were forfeited to the state.[56]

The first phase of the civil wars ended in summer 1646, when the last field army of the king surrendered at Stow-on-the-Wold. The royalist commander, Sir Jacob Astley, presciently remarked: 'You have done your work, boys, and may go and play, unless you will fall out among yourselves.'[57] Meanwhile, there was more work to be done but around the conference table rather than on the battlefield, the challenge of constructing a lasting peace between king and parliament. The peace negotiations dragged on through 1646–47. A complicating factor was that the king, unwilling to surrender himself to the English parliament, had surrendered to the Scots instead. This gave the Scots a massive bargaining chip in their negotiations with the English parliament as they argued the disposition of the king should be decided by both Scottish and English parliaments.[58]

The Scots held the king in custody and offered the royal personage to the English parliamentarians for a price – a cool £1.8 million as payment for their wartime expenses. This was more than parliament was prepared to pay and their accountants set to work. Of the sum demanded, £500,000 was deducted for bed and billeting the Scots during their stay in England. The outstanding sum of £1.3 million was then massaged down to £400,000 to be paid in instalments.[59] However, the Scots were happy and in spring 1647 turned north and began the long march home. But where did the English parliament find the money?

The answer lies in the halls of the worshipful livery companies of the city. These evolved from the ancient trade guilds and were professional bodies that regulated trade and looked after the interests of their members. They were part of the fabric of the city. Admission was achieved after serving an apprenticeship, upon which the applicant became a citizen of London. He could apply to join a livery company and trade. He could vote in elections and stand for office and became liable to pay taxes and could be called upon to serve in a civic office, such as constable. For the politically ambitious, the way upwards was laid out: common councilman, then election to alderman, a senior position. sheriff of the city, then the biggest jump of all to lord mayor.

During the civil wars, the country was governed on two levels: parliament and committee. The parliamentarian war machine was a network of interlocking committees, such as the Committee for the Advance of Money, the Committee for Compounding Delinquents and the Committee for Ejected Ministers. These committees were founded by order of parliament and located in the city. The natural venue for them was the halls of the livery companies. The advantages were obvious: the livery halls were close to parliament at Westminster, thus facilitating speedy communications. Many members of livery companies, particularly the senior members who were masters and wardens, had connections with MPs or were MPs. There was an established hierarchy of literate and numerate personnel who could receive, process and relay instructions and execute the functions of the committee in question.

Initially, the city's contribution to the parliamentarian war effort was through a series of loans. The treasurers of plate and money at Guildhall requested one third of their cash and plate. This was authorised by a parliamentary ordinance on 26 August 1642: *Ordinance for Raising Money in London*.[60] The minds that drafted this ordinance were aware of the possibility of subscribers making token payments, or even non-payment. The ordinance authorised specified assistants to impress upon non-payers the 'Necessity of Subscriptions for Plate and Money', and record the names and amounts pledged to demonstrate their loyalty to the cause.[61] The implied threat was that defaulters would be pressed to make good on their protestations of support. Finally, as an incentive, the ordinance promised subscribers full repayment, plus eight percent interest in trust of the 'Public Faith of the Kingdom', but without specifying a date.[62]

This arrangement might have worked if the civil war had been short and normal business resumed almost immediately. However, after Edgehill, it was obvious the war would be a drawn-out conflict, and any pious hopes to the effect it may have been over by Christmas were dashed. The royalists, at least the wealthy, landed gentry, could finance their war effort by organising subscriptions and selling their plate and other valuables. The king sold honours and imposed a royalist assessment on territories under royalist control. The king also received customs receipts from Bristol, Newcastle and Dartmouth and, later, reluctantly sequestered the estates of captured parliamentarians. [63]

The parliamentarians, who were mainly, but not exclusively, drawn from the ranks of the 'middling sort' leavened with some of the aristocracy, had money and a certain amount of property they could pledge. The poor, who held few assets and relied upon being employed by those above them in the social hierarchy, could of course only offer their services to the cause. This last included church ministers and priests, having taken their oaths of poverty. In November 1642, under the guidance of John Pym, parliament constructed a tax on property and personal wealth, nicknamed the 'Five and Twenty' because those deemed eligible to contribute, i.e. had sufficient wherewithal to pay, were 'requested' to contribute five percent of the value of their property and twenty percent of their personal wealth, in cash, plate or jewellery. This measure was, unsurprisingly, not popular among all the merchants and citizens of London. Not everybody in London was a parliamentarian, and not all parliamentarians in London were prepared to pay. Collection rates varied from ward to ward.

Those who declined to pay were referred to the Committee for Compounding Delinquents, which sat at Goldsmiths' Hall. Originally, this committee sat in Turners' Hall or Guildhall, but soon moved to a permanent base in Goldsmiths' Hall, as this was more convenient for the men of the city who conducted their business at goldsmiths. In time, the committee became known as the Goldsmiths' Hall Committee, as noted in Orders in Parliament on 8 November 1643. [64] Despite its rather imposing name, the committee was a financial committee, not a prosecuting authority. Although cases were referred from the Committee for Raising Money, it acted on instruction from parliament and actions to compound began only after a person was declared to be delinquent. In 1645, however, the committee, under pressure to increase cashflow for the war effort, suggested the innovation of dealing directly with royalists who voluntarily presented themselves to compounding. [65]

During the conflict, this committee had its remit extended to enable them to fine captured royalist officers a sum of money based on the land value of their estates. On payment of the compound, the officer would be released on parole, after first promising not to take arms against parliament again. From the parliamentarian point of view, this idea was ingenious: remove an enemy piece from the chess board and use his money to finance your war effort. The idea was so simple it was brilliant. And it worked. By the summer of 1646, the coffers were overflowing with funds from defeated royalists. The elation at the end of the fighting in summer 1646 was short-lived, however.

Peace negotiations with the king dragged on and on. The army was still mobilised and required payment. Tensions rose in the city. The city that had supported parliament through the war now queried why the New Model Army was still in arms a year after fighting had ceased. The local militias or trained bands were an accepted part of society, but the existence of a national standing army was a new and uncomfortable idea. Taxes continued at their wartime levels, prompting resentment, demonstration and civic unrest. In one spectacular example of civic unrest, the excise house in Smithfield was burnt down.[66] Parliament was getting jittery at the falling away of support:

> *Be it Declared, Ordered, and Ordained, by the Lords and Commons in Parliament assembled, That no Person whatsoever, that hath been in Arms against the Parliament, or hath been aiding or assisting the Forces of the Enemy, or hath been or is sequestered, shall be elected, constituted mayor, alderman, Bailiff, sheriff, Justice of Peace, Steward, of any Court, Constable, or any other Officer, in any County, City, Borough, or Town corporate, within the Kingdom of England, Dominion of Wales, and Town of Berwick: And in case any such Persons as aforesaid be elected into any of the offices aforesaid, in any of the aforesaid Places, the Lords and Commons do declare all such Elections to be void and null: Provided, That this shall not extend to any Person or Persons who have been, or shall be, unduly sequestered as Delinquents, and have been, or shall be, therefore discharged of the said undue Sequestration, by both Houses of Parliament, or by the Lords and Commons for Sequestrations.[67]*

On 6 December 1648, Colonel Thomas Pride, assisted by Lord Grey of Groby, removed those members of parliament thought to be friendly to the idea of a personal treaty with the king from sitting in parliament. This became known as 'Pride's Purge' and the depleted Houses of Commons and Lords that survived the purge was later nicknamed 'The Rump'.[68] The purge of the common council and aldermanic bench in the city on 21 December 1648 is the little-known sequel to Pride's Purge. The newly purged parliament ordered this. Thus, those common councillors and aldermen who either favoured or were even suspected of preferring a personal treaty between the city and the king, were disbarred from standing:

> *Whereas there is an Ordinance of the Lords and Commons assembled in Parliament, bearing date the 18 December, 1648, for the choosing of the common council-men, and other Officers within the City of London and*

the liberties thereof for the year ensuing. The said Lords and Commons do further Declare and Ordained, and bee it hereby Ordained by the said Lords and Commons, that no person whatsoever that subscribed, promoted or abetted, any engagement in the Year 1648, relating to a personal Treaty with the King at London, shall be elected chosen, or put into any of the Offices or places expressed in the aforesaid Ordinance under the penalty contained in the same upon the other excepted persons, and to be levied according to the provision of the said Ordinance; and the lord mayor for the time being is hereby required that this Ordinance with the other bee published at all Elections, and strictly and punctually observed according to the true intent and meaning hereof.[69]

Why was so much effort placed on bringing the City of London back to heel? Quite simply, London was the capital. If news spread that the city was prepared to make a personal treaty with the king, others might follow suit. It would destroy any potential peace settlement as town and county vied to obtain the best terms. Worse still, it would make parliament redundant. Although the city had been a loyal backer of parliament from 1642 to 1646, then a somewhat cooler supporter from 1646 to 1648, the game had changed. As the year 1648 waned, the city's importance in the civil wars waxed. From the point of view of the men who sat in the purged parliament and the army, re-securing the support of the city by whatever means was now a priority.

Although this sounds undemocratic to modern minds, it was an effective strategy. The radical or independent faction of the army now controlled parliament, and any potential opposition from the Presbyterian City of London had been neutralised. This action wasn't universally popular in the city, but the city fathers realised the reality of the situation and fell into step with parliament. Over the next dozen years, the English government saw several changes in name and format. Following the execution of Charles in January 1649, England was successively declared a Commonwealth then a protectorate. Both were just fancy names to describe the republic, or interregnum. Prince Charles, now resident on Jersey, had been declared Charles II in Scotland. The purged parliament lumbered on until the Nominated Assembly, or 'barebones' parliament replaced it. That body was itself finally dissolved by the intervention of Oliver Cromwell. Cromwell reluctantly accepted the role of lord protector, and between 1653 and 1659 three protectorate parliaments sat. Meanwhile, the City of London elected its common councilmen and other officers as before the civil wars.

Chapter 4

Mercers and other livery companies

The parliamentarians' control of London and its resources such as wealth and personnel, plus facilities such as the Tower of London, the Armouries and the Royal Mint, was a vital factor in deciding the outcome of the civil wars. Had the city opted to support the king from the outset, or even abstained from the conflict, the history of the civil war years would almost certainly be very different.[1] But how to manage and optimise this huge resource and ensure the great, complex, machine that was London was working for and not against the parliamentarian cause? The answer lies in committees. Committees for raising money, committees for enforcing non-payers, committees for everything. The natural home for these committees was the city livery companies.

Livery companies were the successors to the ancient trade guilds, whose distant origins evolved from religious orders. They were a combination of a professional standards body and trades union for their members. They regulated business within their specialism and looked after their members' interests. To join a livery company you first had to become a citizen. The usual route to this was via an apprenticeship. On completing your apprenticeship and obtaining your articles, you were eligible to become a citizen of London. To practice your trade, you joined the appropriate livery company. With citizenship came privilege and responsibility. The privilege was your right to vote in elections and stand as candidate for common council. Your responsibility was to practice your trade honestly and diligently, and contribute to the city by taking your turn at a civic office, such as constable. If you were elected as a common councillor and served well, the way was open, theoretically, for you to rise through the ranks to alderman, a senior councillor. If you were fortunate and had good connections, it was possible to rise to the dizzy height of sheriff or Lord Mayor of London.[2]

During the 1630s, the city livery companies had an erratic relationship with the king.[3] On the one hand they owed their charters and monopolies to the crown. This was important. Monopolies were an essential way of regulating business, to ensure that trade did not degenerate into a free-for-all.[4] On the other hand, some of the king's actions upset the livery companies.

Almost all of them had a stake in the Ulster Plantation, the city's asset interest in Ireland. There was a running dispute between the city and the crown over the management of the colony.[5] These issues were finally patched up with a new city charter.[6] However, when the king demanded a loan to finance his wars in Scotland, the city merchants were cautious and deliberately loaned him less than the sum demanded, and much less than they were prepared to pay. There were two reasons behind this: firstly, scepticism about the king's ability or willingness to repay the loan, but secondly and more importantly, the city merchants were seasoned businessmen who knew to only negotiate from a position of strength. In default of topping up his funds from other sources, the king would be forced to recall parliament.

In the long run, the pessimism of the city merchants regarding fulfilment of the king's loan was justified. The royal debt was eventually written off, in the king's mind, but not in the memory of his creditors, nor in the ledgers of the livery companies themselves. The big twelve companies, having been prevailed upon to make a proportionately larger donation than the smaller livery companies, naturally took the lion's share of the hit. Small wonder then that when the crunch came and civil war broke out in England in August 1642, the city's livery companies, royalists and neutrals notwithstanding, declared for parliament. As previously mentioned, the livery companies had organised hierarchies. Their members and the companies had money and manpower. There was an established merchant-bureaucracy in place that could be commandeered for a wartime administration. Their livery halls made first class venues for committees to sit. Last but not least, they were natural recruiting grounds for the City of London trained bands, which was the nucleus of the London Regiments in London and the south-east.

At the corner of Foster Lane and Gresham Street there is an imposing stone building in the classical style. This is the livery hall of the Worshipful Company of Goldsmiths, the fifth most important in the hierarchy of the city livery companies.[7] During the 1630s, there was what modern commentators call a recession. In the seventeenth century, however, there was little comprehension of the economy as it is known today. What was understood was 'decay of trade', which was the term used to describe economic recession in the early seventeenth century. Many factors, including the Thirty Years War, caused this recession, which choked the import and export markets.[8] This restricted the export of English goods like finished cloth and the corresponding inflow of foreign gold. The reduced circulation of gold caused the home economy to stagnate and the market for fancy goods and commodities declined for a while. Although the bigger, wealthier livery companies had more resources to weather the financial storm, on a pound for pound basis they suffered proportionately more than smaller companies. The goldsmiths suddenly found they had unemployed apprentices and journeymen making fancy goods fewer could afford to buy. During the 1630s, this situation rumbled on and gradually the economy cleared. Meanwhile, the unemployed apprentices, bound to the company by their indentures, had re-trained as clerks. This was significant in the civil wars, when London declared for parliament and a multitude of committees was created to deal with the bureaucracy of its war machine.

The Lords and Commons Committee for Compounding Delinquents, to give it its full title, sat at the livery hall of the goldsmiths. Delinquents were first defined as anybody who had not readily and freely given to the parliamentary requests for money. Later this meant captured royalists.[9] We have already seen that the Committee for Compounding raised ample funds from its work to pay off the Scots army in 1646. The goldsmiths must have wished the committee could clear their own financial deficit so easily. The formation of the Ulster Plantation in 1609, to which the goldsmiths contributed, cost £52,000.[10] Four livery companies, the goldsmiths, armourers, cordwainers – who were leatherworkers and bootmakers – and painter-stainers were given land in Derry. This was nothing less than a colony of London merchants in Ireland and the name Londonderry was coined.[11] The goldsmiths were also financially stretched in the 1630s. Whilst navigating their way through the recession, the goldsmiths needed to build a second hall as they had now outgrown the first. This second hall was built in 1634–36, after overcoming several difficulties. The company was required to pay a licence to the king for rebuilding. This wasn't unreasonable as the company was utilising the services of the aptly named Nicholas Stone, the king's mason, and Inigo Jones, the king's surveyor. When the new building stones were delivered, however, they were seized in the king's name and the company was forced to purchase more.[12] Throughout the later 1630s, the company was also trying to find funds to pay its share of ship money, and it is no surprise that in 1637 the goldsmiths were obliged to sell thirty-four pieces of plate, with the intention of reimbursing the members who donated it with replacements when financially stable.[13]

In 1640, the king's demand for a loan from the city of £200,000 for his Scottish wars was reduced to £50,000, of which the goldsmiths' contribution was £3,500. To put that into context, using the formula quoted in the introduction, the goldsmiths' contribution of £3,500 is estimated to be the equivalent of £572,000 nowadays.[14] In June 1642, the city was asked for another loan, this time it was parliament requesting £100,000 for the relief of Ireland. The goldsmiths contributed £7,000 and this was increased by the cost of providing a fire engine, ladders and buckets for the city. Finding twice the amount of money demanded in 1640 was no simple task. The now imminent threat of war saw many merchants' houses closed and the beadle reported he was unable to collect quarterage. Like other livery companies, their cache of weapons had been catalogued and commandeered for the Earl of Essex's army. The attics of the Goldsmiths' Hall were cleared for storage of grain, a wise precaution against the possibility of supply lines to London being cut.[15]

The Armourers and Braziers Hall is located at the northern end of Coleman Street just by the London Wall. Founded as The Guild of St George of the Armourers by ordinance of the lord mayor and aldermen in the year 1322[16], the Worshipful Company of Armourers received their first charter under Henry VI in 1453. Elizabeth I reviewed and ratified their charter in 1559, and in 1619, James I granted them sole control over manufacturers of brass and copper items, edged tools, small firearms and armour on payment of a £100 fine. After the turbulent events of the civil war and restoration, their charter issued in 1619 was belatedly confirmed by James II in 1685. In 1708, Queen Anne issued another charter. This authorised the amalgamation of the armourers with the braziers and granted the new Company of Armourers and Braziers sole rights over armour and weapons makers and workers in copper and brass, within 11 miles of London[17]. During their early history, the armourers joined with other companies in related trades. The fourbers, who refurbished old armour, joined in 1387, and the heaumers, helmet-makers, in the fifteenth century. When in 1575 the armourers absorbed the bladesmiths, this caused friction with the cutlers and sheathers companies. All three were involved in the manufacture of knives and each claimed the rights of search. However, the dispute was resolved and it was agreed each company would supervise its own members.[18]

As a city livery company, the armourers were required to provide a quota of men for the London trained bands as directed by the lord mayor. However, their role in the manufacture of weapons and armour gave them special status. This exempted them from supplying more than a handful of men for military service as their craft in the armouries was a higher priority.[19] In 1631, business picked up under the warlike King Charles, when the company was contracted to make 1,600 suits of armour per month and their best craftsmen were seconded to the Royal Armoury at Greenwich[20]. During the uneasy summer of 1642, the House of Lords, anticipating war with the king, kept close tabs on various city livery companies and the resources they could offer:

> *Ordered, That the Master and Wardens of the Saddlers, Bit-makers,*
> *Gun-makers, and Armourers, shall attend To-morrow, to give an Account,*
> *according to the former Order of this House, what Arms and Saddles, &c.*
> *are bespoke, &c.*[21]

As well as producing armour such as breastplates for the armies, the armourers also provided quarter to the soldiery that inhabited London throughout the civil wars. Like other livery companies, the armourers took precautions against billeted soldiers either commandeering or simply helping themselves to the company's plate and valuables. In January 1648, the Court of Assistants ordered that, in the event of soldiers being quartered at their hall, the master and wardens should remove the company's plate to a secret hiding place. The Court of Assistants approved this anticipatory measure and further ordered that the master and wardens should disclose to the court where the plate was hidden and produce it when requested to do so.[22]

Just across Gresham Street stood the livery hall of the Worshipful Company of Haberdashers. The haberdashers received their ordinances from the lord mayor in 1371, and were incorporated by a royal charter from Henry VI in 1461.[23] Like many buildings, Haberdashers' Hall did not survive the restoration. It was destroyed in the Fire of London in 1666, a fate the second hall shared when it burnt down in an air-raid in 1940.[24] The company moved to their present hall in Smithfield in 2002 and the site in Gresham Street is now occupied by Lloyd's Bank[25]. Yet the nearby property marker reminds us that here was the hall of one of the most militant livery companies in London during the civil war years. During these years, the haberdashers hosted the Committee for the Advance of Money. This was logical as their hall stood at the corner of Gresham Street and Staining Lane, a stone's throw from where the Committee for Compounding sat in Goldsmiths' Hall and near the Guildhall.

The Committee for the Advance of Money was headed by Edward Howard, Baron Escrick. Lord Howard had dubious credentials for a future parliamentarian committeeman. Elected MP for the seats of Wallingford and Calne in 1624, he chose to represent the borough of Calne. Howard appears to have drifted in and out of politics. He was member for Calne in the 1624 and 1625 parliaments but absent from the 1626 parliament.

He returned to the Commons as MP for Hertford in 1628. However, his parliamentary career was quiet and Howard appears to have confined himself to the backbenches. In April 1628, he was raised to the peerage as Baron Escrick and assumed his seat in the Lords.[26] We know little of his activities in the 1630s, but in 1640 he evidently started taking more interest in politics. Howard was one of the twelve nobles who presented Charles with their list of grievances at York in 1640 and voted against the king's supply in the short parliament. He served on a multitude of committees during the civil war: Committee for the Advance of Money in 1642; the Committee of Both Kingdoms 1643–48, Admiralty Committee and the Committee of Westminster Divines 1643; Committee for Compounding 1647; Council of State 1650; and many others. The year 1649 saw the English government dramatically reformatted. Both houses of parliament had been purged in December 1648. The restructuring of English politics continued in January 1649, when the Commons dispensed with the House of Lords. With no Upper House to sit in, Howard returned to the Commons as member for Carlisle. However, in 1651 Howard's political career ended when he was discharged from both positions after being exposed for taking bribes from royalist supporters. Howard died in 1675 and was buried in the Savoy Chapel.[27]

In 1643, the Worshipful Company of Haberdashers purchased 150 muskets for the parliamentarian cause.[28] The haberdashers were one of the most radical companies in the city and the depth of their generosity is remarkable. In the early months, new supplies of weapons were urgently needed and both sides resorted to importing them. However, there were complaints about the efficiency of imported muskets and parliament ordered these be tested before being issued:

> *Ordered, That the Petition of the Gunmakers, desiring, "That such Muskets as come from Foreign Parts may be tried before they be used, because divers Men have been hurt by the breaking of Muskets:" Hereupon this House Ordered, That the said Petition is committed to the Committee for the Safety.*[29]

The shortfall in the production of weapons may partly be due to the blocked imports of sea-coal into London, which by 1643 was affecting not only domestic heating but also impacted upon those industries like glass-making and gun manufacture that required a ready supply of heat.[30] The coal blockade also introduced an inflation wave into London. Scarcity of coal pushed its price up and therefore increased the prices of every commodity whose manufacture or sale depended on coal or was related to coal. Wood was resorted to but wood tends to burn more quickly than coal and doesn't necessarily produce sufficient heat that industrial processes require. Worse still, in another knock-on effect, the rapid usage of supplies of wood for burning in and around London made that commodity more expensive and, as an emergency reaction in October 1643, with a bitter winter looming, parliament authorised the cutting of wood from estates of royalists, delinquents and church lands within 60 miles of London.[31] Allowing for this inflation wave, the haberdashers' contribution of 150 muskets in 1643 was generous and costly. The haberdashers never recouped the money loaned to the parliamentarian cause.[32]

The Worshipful Company of Tallow Chandlers and its more upmarket sister, the Worshipful Company of Wax Chandlers, were both candle-makers. However, there were two kinds of candles. Tallow candles were used by poorer people because they were cheap. They were made out of animal fat and, as well as being more affordable, were smelly and unreliable as light sources because they tended to gutter and flare, depending on the quality of the animal fat used in their manufacture. Wax candles on the other hand were used by the wealthy and the powerful, which included merchants and their livery companies, the church, the Corporation of London, parliament and the court.[33] Wax candles were more expensive but more reliable than tallow candles because they were made out of beeswax, not animal fat. The wax chandlers obtained their ordinance in 1371 and in 1484 received their royal charter, the only known charter issued to a city livery company by Richard III. The company purchased its operative charter from Charles II in 1663.[34] The wax chandlers have owned the land on Gresham Street, where their present hall stands, since 1501.[35] Although candles were an everyday staple in the seventeenth century, the fortunes of the wax chandlers declined during the civil war years. Demand for candles fluctuated. The anti-Laudian reforms of the Harley Committee meant a sharp drop in the demand for candles used in churches, offset by higher usage of candles in parliament. However, the tallow chandlers didn't suffer so much, possibly because their products were cheaper than those sold by their upmarket rivals.

Tucked away on the corner of Cheapside and Ironmonger Lane lies the Hall of the Worshipful Company of Mercers. Mercers were dealers in fine cloth, an important product of the English market at home and abroad. The Worshipful Company of Mercers is the most important livery company in the City of London. The mercers received their ordinances in 1347 and their first royal charter from Richard II in 1393. The mercers' charter was called in and re-issued by Mary I in 1558, and this was renewed, without alterations, by Elizabeth I in 1559 and James I in 1611.[36] This charter of 1611 remained in place until 1684, when it was surrendered to Charles II. Their charter was not inspected by Charles I, although during the Commonwealth there was a parliamentary committee reviewing charters issued to corporations. In November 1652, the wardens were instructed to present their charter to the committee, although it appears that no changes were made.[37] During the civil war years, the mercers absorbed heavy losses to the king and parliament, as London historian Walter Thornbury narrates:

> *During the civil wars both King and Parliament bore heavily on the Mercers. In 1640 Charles I. half forced from them a loan of £3,030, and in 1642 the Parliament borrowed £6,500, and arms from the Company's armoury, valued at £88. They afterwards gave further arms, valued at £71 13s. 4d., and advanced as a second loan £3,200.*[38]

Three companies were related by their trades: The Worshipful Companies of Saddlers (saddle-makers), Farriers and Loriners. These were three separate companies, but in our survey of the civil war their contribution may be considered collectively. The trade of saddlers needs no explanation, but that of farrier and loriner may be unfamiliar. Farriers were men who fitted horseshoes, a very important trade when the horse was the only realistic means of travel. Farriers should not be conflated with blacksmiths, despite their similar trades. Blacksmiths work metal at a forge, as does the farrier when making horseshoes. However, the farrier is also concerned with the care and wellbeing of the horse.[39] Loriners manufacture bits, bridles, spurs and stirrups, in other words the various components that make up a horse's harness.[40] Thus it can be seen these were very important trades. It took three people practising different trades to equip one horse. Each of these three trades is practised today, even in the age of motorised transport there is still a need for horses. The saddlers owned property in Westcheap and later built their livery hall in Gutter Lane. The loriners plied their trade at the east end of Cheapside. The farriers date their origin back to 1356, when Lord Mayor Henry Pickford called upon the farriers of the city to establish standards of training and workmanship.[41] Despite their longstanding as a guild, when the Orders of Precedence for the livery companies were drawn up in 1515, the saddlers were ranked twenty-fifth.

The 1630s was a difficult period for the saddlers. Outbreaks of plague in 1629–31 and in 1635 interrupted the company's business. This was compounded by the company's struggle to maintain its monopoly of trade. There was a continual threat that the coach-harness-makers might form their own company and the saddlers would lose business. This was a long-running issue. A petition to parliament in 1602 and a wave of prosecutions in the 1620s and 1630s failed to address the problem. In 1635, the star chamber ordered the number of coaches in London be limited. Within the company, internal disciplinary action was taken against senior members who, in 1635 and 1639, took their goods to trade fairs without the wardens' permission, which was against their rules of incorporation.[42] Further external pressures followed with the bishops' wars of 1639/40, when Charles demanded a loan of £200,000 to finance his army. The city reduced this to £50,000 and the saddlers were tasked with contributing £600.[43] A year later, in 1641, Charles had made peace with his northernmost kingdom and on his return to London was feasted and fêted. The saddlers' part was to provide ten men for the king's escort party, and two senior members, William Pease and William Kettle, acted as the king's servants at table during the lavish banquet organised by Lord Mayor Richard Gurney.[44]

However, this rosy picture of reconciliation and royal favour did not last. In the autumn of 1641, the Irish rebellion hit the Ulster Plantation and many colonists were killed or dispossessed. The city's response was those companies with a stake in the plantation to assist and the saddlers sent twenty quarters of wheat and £20. Later, the city asked the saddlers for a further £1,200, of which, after some negotiation, £1,000 was paid. The saddlers were not being mean, it was cashflow not callousness. Their portion was financed by taking out a loan for £900 and selling company silverware to find the remaining £100.[45] During the emergency stock-take of weapons in the city in August 1642, the saddlers supplied sixteen muskets and sixteen swords and belts, and paid £200, which was the accrued balance of their loan for the relief of the Ulster Plantation. This, however, was the least of their contribution to parliament's war effort. An ordinance of 1 November 1642 allowed apprentices to enlist in the army without breaking their indentures and guaranteed their eligibility to resume their apprenticeship after the war ended, assuming, of course, they survived:

Whereas, in Times of common Danger and Necessity, the Interest of private Persons ought to give Way to the Public; it is Ordained and Declared, by the Lords and Commons in Parliament, That such Apprentices as have been, or shall be, listed to serve as Soldiers for the Defence of the Religion and Liberty of the Kingdom, His Majesty's Royal Person, the Parliament, and the city of London, their Sureties and such as stand engaged for them shall be secured, against their masters, their Executors, and Administrators, from all Loss and Inconvenience, by Forfeiture of Bonds, Covenants, Enfranchisements, or otherwise; and that, after this Public Service ended, the masters of such Apprentices shall be commanded and required to receive them again into their Service, without imposing upon them any Punishment, Loss, or Prejudice, for their absence in the Defence of the Commonwealth: And the Lords and Commons do further Declare, That, if it shall appear that the masters of such Apprentices have received any considerable Loss by the Absence of their Apprentices, they will take Care that reasonable Satisfaction shall be made unto them, out of the Public Stock of the Kingdom according to Justice and Indifference.[46]

Meanwhile, London was being fortified as the king was expected to attack his capital. The saddlers boarded up their windows and purchased fire-fighting equipment. This was a general precaution against fire. For the saddlers, however, the risk was specific as their hall was used to store gunpowder.[47] Business and company life continued. Company dinners still took place, although these were necessarily restricted and scaled down.[48] On the plus side, business boomed. However, the business model of supplying the parliamentarian armies meant large contracts with the smaller manufacturers of components acting as subcontractors.[49] Thus, those members of the company who were wealthy found themselves wealthier because of their greater resources. Others found themselves under pressure to complete their orders.

The Worshipful Company of Grocers, so named because they sold goods by the gross, found itself under continual pressure to supply funds, as Walter Thornbury notes:

During the Civil War the Grocers suffered, like all their brother companies. In 1645, the Parliament exacted £50 per week from them towards the support of troops, £6 for City defences, and £8 for wounded soldiers. The company had soon to sell £1,000 worth of plate. A further demand for arms, and a sum of £4,500 for the defence of the city, drove them to sell all the rest of their plate, except the value of £300. In 1645, the watchful Committee of Safety, sitting at Haberdashers' Hall, finding the company indebted £500 to one Richard Greenough, a Cavalier delinquent, compelled them to pay that sum.[50]

On the other hand, the generosity of the grocers towards their parliamentarian masters and some-time allies was lavish indeed:

> In 1648, the Grocers had to petition General Fairfax not to quarter his troops in the hall of a charitable company like theirs. In 1649, a grand entertainment was given by the Grocers to Cromwell and Fairfax. After hearing two sermons at Christ's Church, preached by Mr. Goodwin and Dr. Owen, Cromwell, his officers, the speaker, and the judges, dined together. "No drinking of healths," says a Puritan paper of the time, "nor other uncivil concomitants formerly of such great meetings, nor any other music than the drum and trumpet—a feast, indeed, of Christians and chieftains, whereas others were rather of Chretiens and cormorants." The surplus food was sent to the London prisons, and £40 distributed to the poor. The aldermen and Council afterwards went to General Fairfax at his house in Queen Street, and, in the name of the city, presented him with a large basin and ewer of beaten gold; while to Cromwell they sent a great present of plate, value £300, and 200 pieces of gold. They afterwards gave a still grander feast to Cromwell in his more glorious time.[51]

These two contradictory passages sum up the mood of the livery companies and London in general during the civil war years. Willing and happy to support parliament when things were going well, or to obtain favour, but less inclined to shell out in unhappier circumstances. It is also significant that the controversial minister John Goodwin, who had been removed from his home parish of St Stephen, Coleman Street, was invited to preach before the great and the good of the army and the city. By 1649, the independents, political and religious, had gained the upper hand over the Presbyterians, and it's apparent this shift was making its way through the livery companies.

Another city livery company that was negatively impacted by the civil wars was the Worshipful Company of Tobacco Pipe Makers and Tobacco Blenders. The story of tobacco-smoking in England started in 1573, when Sir Francis Drake brought tobacco from the New World of America. The formation of the East India Company in 1601 created an import market for foreign goods, including spices and tobacco. However, James I was anti-smoking and in 1604 published his *Counterblaste to Tobacco* and raised the import duty by a thousand percent. By 1613, there were an estimated 7,000 tobacco sellers in England.[52] The revenue from the import duty was being undercut by domestic tobacco-growing and smuggling. Although James was anti-smoking, he rather enjoyed spending the revenue collected from the imposition of tobacco duty. In order to regulate and police the tobacco trade, in 1619, James ordered that all tobacco be imported through London and a single company of pipe-makers in Westminster be formed to hold the monopoly. Charles renewed their charter in 1634 and renamed the company the Tobacco-pipe Makers of London and Westminster and England and Wales. The tobacco-makers received their status as a city company. They had no livery hall, but met in the halls of other livery companies. This period of the tobacco-makers' history, 1619 to 1643, is known as the First Company. The financial strain of the civil wars was too heavy for the company, however. The tobacco-makers could not afford to pay their annual fine to the king and Charles cancelled their charter. The company was reformed by the City of London in 1660 and re-incorporated by a royal charter of Charles II in 1663. This second incorporation therefore became known as the Second Company.[53]

The Worshipful Company of Cutlers manufactured and sold not only fine cutlery for use at table, but also produced swords and daggers for ceremonial and military use. A *Gild* of Cutlers was recorded as working near Cheapside in the year 1285, and in the year 1344 they were officially recognised by an ordinance of the mayor and aldermen, giving the guild the right of search and assay on cutlery produced within the city.[54] Their first royal charter was issued by Henry V in 1416 and confirmed not only their right of search and assay but also allowed the cutlers to own property directly instead of through trustees. This was a rare honour as the cutlers are the only city livery company known to receive a charter from Henry V.[55] In the early sixteenth century, the cutlers, like other livery companies, had grown and this led to disputes about their position in the Order of Precedence. In the year 1515, the livery companies were placed into order, determined by their wealth at the time, and the cutlers are number eighteen in the Order of Precedence. They received their latest charter from James I in 1606.[56] Nowadays, Cutlers' Hall is at the north end of Warwick Lane, but during the civil war years their hall was in Cloak Lane, where Cannon Street Station now is. The company moved to its present premises in 1888, when the Metropolitan and District Railway obtained a compulsory purchase order.[57]

During the early years of the civil war, the cutlers were impeded by the relative lack and high expense of sourcing both coal and steel for their products. The civil war period, with its increased demand for swords and belts, was, however, vital to the wellbeing of the cutlers. The 1630s with its decay of trade had hit this company hard. In March 1636, the company was in debt and attempting to pay its share of ship money, provision of corn for

Ireland, and a precept issued for the repair of St Paul's Cathedral, and they were obliged to sell their plate for £60. In 1638, the king demanded a further £80 and this was funded by calling sixteen new liverymen, selected by the master and wardens, each required to pay entry fines of £5.[58] In October 1640, the company borrowed £1,000, half of which was immediately loaned to the city for the relief of its asset in Ireland. The introduction of the weekly assessment put further strain upon the coffers of the cutlers, and to ease their cashflow, £200-worth of plate was sold in May 1643. Fortunately for the cutlers, in May 1645 the city repaid £180, which was about one third of the original £500 loaned in October 1640.[59]

The Worshipful Company of Stationers were also affected by the civil war, but somewhat differently compared to other livery companies. The stationers' specialism was not supply of goods, it was enforcement of copyright and censorship.

In July 1643, John Pym made what was possibly his greatest contribution to the parliamentarian war effort when he suggested a national excise tax. This idea was taken up and, on 22 July 1643, an ordinance was passed with the long-winded title:

> *July 1643: An Ordinance for the speedy Rising and Levying of Moneys, set by way of Charge or new Impost, on the several Commodities mentioned in the Schedule hereunto annexed; As well for the better securing of Trade, as for the maintenance of the Forces raised for the Defence of the King and Parliament, both by Sea and Land, as for and towards the Payment of the Debts of the Common-wealth, for which the Public Faith is, or shall be given.*[60]

The Excise Ordinance, as this was later known, included a schedule of taxable commodities and the applicable rate of duty payable. For instance:

> *In this Schedule is contained the Charge and Excise which by the ordinance hereunto annexed is set and imposed, to be paid on the several Commodities hereafter mentioned. Inprimis, for every pound of Tobacco, which is not of the English Plantation, over and above all Customs due for the same, to be paid by the first buyer thereof from the Merchant or Importer, four shillings. Item, for every pound of Tobacco of the English plantation abroad, or made in the Land, over and above all Customs due for the same, to be paid by the first buyer thereof, from the Merchant or Importer, two shillings. Item, for every Tonne of Wine containing four Hogsheads, being*

here retailed over and above all Customs due for the same, to be paid by the
first retailor thereof, and so after that rate for a lesser or greater quantity,
six pounds. Item, for every Tonne of Wine here bought for private use, over
and above all Customs due for the same, to be paid by the first buyer from
the Merchant, three pounds.[61]

This schedule contains some interesting points. Note the duty on foreign produced tobacco is double that of tobacco grown by English planters, early indicators of protecting the home market. Further entries in the schedule refer specifically to duty payable on imports of Dutch and Spanish commodities. Secondly, wine purchased for personal use was taxed at half the rate of wine bought for selling on. How it was enforced that a purchaser of wine for 'private use' would not sell it is unclear. The ordinance also sets out that commissioners, clerks and 'subordinate officers' will be appointed to maintain registers of merchants and ensure that accounts were submitted promptly, and to employ powers of search and seizure with authority to call in the trained bands if resisted. The commissioners were to be appointed by the Committee for Advance of Money, but the ordinance specified that John Langham, sheriff of the City of London, was to be appointed treasurer of the London Excise Office.[62] The ordinance actually states 'John Longham', but there is no trace of a John Longham serving as sheriff, and this is almost certainly a misspelling.

John Langham was a noted member of the Levant and Far-East Companies, where he made his wealth. During the civil war years, he commanded a city regiment, but his Presbyterian outlook turned him against the New Model Army, a stance that earned him a spell of imprisonment in the Tower in 1647. He served on two civil war committees: treasurer for the excise in 1643; and as trustee for Bishops' Lands in 1646. He sat as MP for London in 1654 and Southwark in 1660, while secretly funding royalists, another example of the trimmers. In 1660, he was raised to the rank of baronet for his service in assisting with the restoration. However, he was now in his mid-70s and retired from public life. He died in 1671 and was buried in his manor at Cottesbrooke, which he had purchased in 1639.[63]

Chapter 5

Religious strife

I f you were to walk west along Cheapside in the early 1640s you would
come across a strikingly tall obelisk, approximately 30 feet tall. It
was shaped like a cross and was covered in an ornate lead moulding
to protect it from the elements. This was the Cheapside Cross, one of
the famous Eleanor Crosses erected by King Edward I in memory of
his beloved wife, Eleanor of Castile, after her untimely death in the late
thirteenth century.[1] For over 300 years the crosses stood as a memorial
of Christian piety. That was in the Middle Ages, this was now in the
uncertain religious atmosphere of the 1640s. Following the reformation of
the 1500s, religious icons were viewed with equal suspicion or veneration,
depending which side of the religious divide you were. Altars in churches
were stripped, images covered up or hidden away. Anything that harked
back to the superstitions of the medieval Roman Catholic church was
suspect.

During the early phase of the civil wars, the Eleanor Crosses and
similar constructs, such as Paul's Cross, where sermons were preached
and news of great events such as royal births or marriages or declarations
of war was announced, received their death warrants.[2] Their judge was the
Committee for Demolition of Monuments of Superstition and Idolatry,
created by the Commons on 24 April 1643. The appointed 'executioner'
was a hard-line puritan and anti-Catholic parliamentarian officer, Sir
Robert Harley. This committee would hence be referred to as the Harley
Committee.[3]

> *This Committee is to receive Information, from time to time, of
> any Monuments of Superstition or Idolatry in the Abbey church at
> Westminster, or the Windows thereof, or in any other church or chapel, in
> or about London: And they have Power to demolish the same, where any
> such superstitious or idolatrous Monuments are informed to be: And all
> churchwardens, and other Officers, are hereby required to be aiding and
> assisting in the Execution of this Order: And are to meet at Two a Clock
> this Afternoon, in the Exchequer Chamber.*[4]

Sir Robert was the ideal choice to head this committee. A strict puritan, he had previously supported parliamentary motions in 1626 to demolish the Cheapside Cross.[5] On 2 May 1643, Sir Robert achieved this when the Cheapside Cross, known then as Westcheap Cross, was demolished by order of the common council.[6] The city fathers were impatient at the speed at which parliament was implementing religious reform. On 23 January 1641, Isaac Penington, alderman and MP for the City of London, pressured the Commons to action and threatened to withhold a proposed loan of £60,000.[7] The Lords had recently written to the City of London and, in a well-meant attempt to prevent unseemly disturbances in churches, offered to accommodate innovations in religion. Naturally, this proposal infuriated the puritans and a conference to discuss the feasibility of removing religious imagery from churches was called. The proposed conference was overtaken by discussion in parliament, which eventually passed the Commons Order for the Suppression of Innovations [in religion] in September 1641.[8] In the eighteen months or so that parliament sat before the civil wars, there was always too much business and too little time to discuss it, and even the most pressing issues awaiting legislation simply had to wait their turn. This did not improve after the outbreak of the civil wars as the Westminster parliament was now carrying out all business, but with reduced personnel.

In spring 1643, the city fathers lost patience and ordered the Cheapside Cross to be demolished, and this galvanised parliament into action when they appointed the Harley Committee. Historically, this was a dramatic sea-change in policy, as previously the city had cared for and maintained the cross, as the Records of the City Remembrancers note:

> *In the centre of Cheapside, just opposite Wood Street, stood the Cross, one of the series erected by Edward the First to his Queen Eleanor, Daughter of Alphonso, King of Castile. It was built by Michael de Cantuaria in 1291– 3, at a cost of 226l. 13s. 4d. It was long the care of the Citizens, and was rebuilt in 1441, and regilt at the coming of the Emperor, Charles the Fifth, in 1522. It was broken and defaced as an object of the Romish religion in 1581; repaired in 1595; again, defaced in 1600, and finally destroyed in the Mayoralty of Sir Isaac Pennington, May 2nd, 1643.[9]*

Popular portrayals of that dramatic day paint a picture of a scene reminiscent of a political rally. Two regiments of the London trained bands lined the streets, as much for crowd-control and to beat off any royalist opposition. Ropes attached to the cross were tightened. The soldiers, flushed with excitement, took the strain. Sir Robert Harley, sitting astride his horse, gave the order. Over and again the soldiers tugged on the ropes, sweating and grunting with the exertion. Eventually, might prevailed over metal, and the cross toppled and smashed, followed by a huge cheer.

Notwithstanding the popular images of this taking place, it is somewhat unlikely the cross was simply pulled down, as happened to statues of Saddam Hussein after the Arab Spring. The thick, ornate lead moulding would have protected the cross from more than just rain, thunder and frost. It was like a suit of armour. It is more likely the lead was stripped away beforehand. At which point the cross may well have been dramatically pulled down, or less romantically simply dismantled with hammer and crowbar. One burning question remains though. What happened to the lead moulding that was carefully stripped away? The best explanation is that this precious commodity, whose precise weight is unknown but may be estimated at several hundred pounds, was not wasted. It was almost certainly melted down and recast into musket balls, as Dr Julie Spraggon notes.[10] Londoners have always been recyclers and it is unlikely this free resource would be overlooked. Waste not, want not. Meanwhile, the Harley Committee continued its work with zeal, boosted by further instructions in May 1644, 'An ordinance for the further demolition of Monuments of Idolatry and Superstition', which ordered the following:

> *That all Representations of any of the Persons of the Trinity, or of any Angel or Saint, in or about any cathedral, Collegiate or parish church, or chapel, or in any open place within this Kingdome, shall be taken away, defaced, and utterly demolished; And that no such shall hereafter be set up, And that the Chancel - ground of every such church or chapel, raised for any Altar, or Communion Table to stand upon, shall be laid down and levelled; And that no Copes, Surplices, superstitious Vestments, Roods, or Roodlons, or Holy-water Fonts, shall be, or be any more used in any church or chapel within this Realm; And that no Cross, Crucifix, Picture, or Representation of any of the Persons of the Trinity, or of any Angel or Saint shall be, or continue upon any Plate, or other thing used, or to be used in or about the worship of God.[11]*

The taking down of the Cheapside Cross and similar symbols of idolatry was undoubtedly a dramatic incident in the history of civil war-London. Equally striking, however, was the treatment meted out to St Paul's Cathedral. Old St Paul's had lost its spire in 1571, and the fabric of the cathedral continued to deteriorate until James I took an interest in restoring its condition. However, there were delays, and repair work wasn't commenced until the 1630s.[12] It took the driving personality of William Laud and the genius of king's surveyor Inigo Jones to restore some of St Paul's lost glory. Jones' incomplete restoration was also a remodelling. The cathedral retained its cruciform floor plan, but the houses and shops that had previously thronged round its precincts were removed. The transept was refaced and the west end enhanced with a classical portico. Charles was so impressed he financed the work from his privy purse.[13] However, it is equally likely this was intended to stimulate more generous contributions from the well-heeled in the City of London, as noted in the index to the Remembrancier, the log of letters between central government and the City of London:

> *Letter from the Archbishop of Canterbury (Laud) to the Lord Mayor, &c., forwarding, by desire of the King, copy of His Majesty's letter, in which he had signified his intention of taking upon himself the cost of the repair of the whole west end of the Cathedral; and expressing his hope that the King's great munificence would stir them up to extend their charity. 28th April, 1634.*[14]

However, this restoration work ceased when the civil war broke out in 1642. The restoration fund, £17,000, was commandeered to pay the parliamentarian soldiers. The nave was turned over to stabling for the cavalry, although the Lady Chapel was retained for preaching. In addition to the standard iconoclasm of smashing stained-glass windows, vandalising statues and the burning of carvings, the porch was let out to small traders.[15] St Paul's Cathedral was not singled out for special treatment. Its counterpart in Whitehall, Westminster Abbey, suffered a similar fate, as did many churches and cathedrals, although curiously the old priory church of St Saviour and St Mary Overie, latterly and better known as Southwark Cathedral, was spared.[16]

Like many of the committees created during the civil war years, the Harley Committee was relatively short-lived. Committees were formed for a specific purpose and sat until they had performed their purpose, in which case they were wound up, or replaced with another committee. The Committee of Safety, for example, sat from 1642 until 1644, when it was replaced by the Committee of Both Kingdoms.[17] By contrast, the Harley Committee must have served its purpose as no record of it, or a successor committee after 1646, has been identified. On the other hand, there was a further round of iconoclasm in the early years of the Commonwealth. On 15 February 1649, parliament ordered the king's arms above the speaker's chair to be removed from the Commons. In August 1649, a small committee of three MPs were tasked with removing the king's arms in public places, and in August 1649 this was extended to all ships in the parliamentarian navy and merchant shipping.[18] These measures were not always successfully enforced. In December 1650, Sir Henry Mildmay, MP for Maldon, reported seeing royal icons in various churches, livery halls and public places in the City of London, and urged these be removed at the earliest opportunity. He also reported that the banned festival of Christmas was, despite its illegality, still being observed.[19] Although this report was referred to the Committee for Plundered Ministers, its counterpart, the Harley Committee, was by now defunct. An ordinance of 5 February 1651 ordered the removal of all the king's images and further ordered that the Council of State should oversee and execute the orders, instead of delegating them to a committee.[20]

Sir Henry was an example of those MPs who held offices under the king before the civil wars, but crossed over to the parliamentarians when the crack between king and parliament widened to a gulf in 1642. The offices he was appointed to might have qualified him to be a royalist office-holder for life: master of the king's jewels under King James in 1618, a very prestigious position. Under King Charles, in 1630, he was a commissioner charged with compounding and collecting fines from eligible men who had not presented themselves for knighthoods at the king's coronation. And in 1640, he served as deputy-lieutenant in Essex, where he assisted in collecting the coat-and-conduct money, the army equivalent of the hated ship money.[21] Although in April 1641 Sir Henry ran with the hounds during Earl Strafford's trial, when it came to the crunch he abstained in the vote against Strafford's attainder by hiding in the privy during the parliamentary division.[22] He finally broke with the king some time between then and 1642. He worked actively on various parliamentarian committees throughout the civil wars and afterwards, such as commissioner for the revenue from 1648 to 1652. In 1649, parliament ordered Sir Henry to be repaid £2,000 with interest, from money he had previously loaned the king. Fittingly, for a man that deplored royal and religious imagery, he was paid out of funds acquired by the sale of lands formerly belonging to cathedrals. Whether this was related to his service as a judge at the king's trial in January 1649 is unclear. Sir Henry was tried as a regicide at the restoration, although he didn't sign the king's death warrant and pleaded the defence that he only sat as a judge in order to spare the king's life. This tactic saved his neck, but not his character. He was stripped of his titles, barred from public office, and imprisoned for life. Following a failed escape attempt, he was exiled to Tangier, where he died in 1668.[23]

Another aspect of religious reform during the civil war years was control of the pulpit. If the stained-glass windows, statues and other iconography inside and outside the churches were strong religious propaganda, there was much more powerful propaganda delivered from the pulpit. The removal of scandalous ministers was a priority for both sides. The Committee for Plundered Ministers, initially set-up to compensate puritan ministers ejected and replaced by churchmen more amenable to Laudian principles, now found its remit reversed.[24] Pro-royalist clergy were expelled from their livings in the London parishes, as happened to Benjamin Stone of St Clement Eastcheap in March 1643:

> *An Ordinance for Sequestering the Rents and Profits of the Parsonage of St. Clement next Eastcheap, London, whereof Mr. Ben. Stone is Parson, into the Hands of certain Sequestors named in the said Ordinance, to the Use and Benefit of Mr. Walth. Taylor, a Master of Arts, a godly, learned, and orthodox Divine; who is hereby appointed and required to preach every Lord's Day, and to officiate as Parson, and to take care for the Discharge of the Cure of the said Place, in all the Duties thereof, until further Order shall be taken by both Houses of Parliament.*[25]

This short passage tells us how the process of replacing ministers was carried out and justified. When a minister was ejected from his living, a parliamentary ordinance was issued, demonstrating that due process had been applied. Sequesters were appointed to oversee the handover. Note also how the ordinance tells us virtually nothing about the expelled minister. On the other hand, his replacement is praised for his qualifications and there is an emphasis on his godliness, his learning, and orthodoxy, which implied his predecessor was lacking these qualities and was thus unfit to keep his living. Benjamin Stone had been appointed to the parish of St Clement Eastcheap by William Juxon, Bishop of London, in 1638. Following his ejection, he had a short spell under house-arrest at Crosby Hall, then located in Bishopsgate. Stone retired to Plymouth and on payment of £60 obtained his freedom and appears to have stayed there for remaining the civil war years. Stone returned to his former parish in Eastcheap at the restoration, dying five years later.[26]

For a minister to be ejected from his living and, as in the case of Ben Stone, be required to purchase his freedom, was a bitter financial blow.

However, there was a degree of humanitarian relief for families of the dispossessed clergymen. The wife and children of the ejected minister could claim one-fifth of their former living, payable by the replacement minister. Obviously, this wasn't an ideal arrangement. One-fifth of a living intended for a family would barely support a wife and young children. Furthermore, the new ministers often resented losing twenty percent of their living and frequently delayed payment or even withheld it altogether. In these cases, the Committee for Plundered Ministers found itself stepping in, not only to oversee the changeover, but also to act as a go-between to ensure the new incumbent paid his dues.[27] The Orders and Minute Book of the United Parishes, for example, records that in October 1645, several inhabitants of the parish of St Anne and St Agnes, in Gresham Street, refused to pay their tithes to Mr Love, the rector. Despite protesting their compliance with the will of parliament, the defaulters failed to give a satisfactory explanation and were given seven days to pay the sequesters, after which they would be referred to the Committee for Examination who would enforce payment.[28]

What might mark out a clergyman as a royalist, or even an unreliable supporter of parliament? The most obvious example of a royalist churchman was William Laud, the Archbishop of Canterbury, whose high church reforms in the 1630s rankled with puritans. Laud had been accused of treason by the long parliament in 1640, before the civil wars broke out:

> *That he hath traitorously endeavoured to alter and subvert God's true Religion, by Law established in this Realm, and instead thereof to set up Popish Superstition and Idolatry. And to that end, hath declared and maintained in Speeches, and printed Books, divers Popish Doctrines and Opinions, contrary to the Articles of Religion established by Law. He hath urged and enjoined divers Popish and Superstitious Ceremonies without any warrant of Law, and hath cruelly persecuted those who have opposed the same, by corporal Punishments and Imprisonments, and most unjustly vexed others, who refused to conform thereunto, by Ecclesiastical Censures of Excommunication, Suspension, Deprivation, and Degradation, contrary to the Laws of this Kingdom.[29]*

The combined articles accusing Laud of treason were collated by the Commons and presented to the Lords by John Pym on 26 February 1641.[30] Laud was also accused of treason in his role of Archbishop of Canterbury in the grand remonstrance of 1641. The grand remonstrance was a document compiled and also presented by John Pym that itemised the ills of the country. In essence, it was a petition from parliament to the king and contained over

200 grievances.[31] After the usual lengthy preamble, the ills of the kingdom were laid out. Religious grievances came first:

> *That you will be graciously pleased to concur with the humble Desires of your People in a Parliamentary Way, for the preserving the Peace and Safety of the Kingdom from the malicious Designs of the Popish Party. For depriving the bishops of their Votes in Parliament, and abridging their immoderate Power usurped over the Clergy, and other your good Subjects, which they have perniciously abused, to the Hazard of Religion, and great Prejudice and Oppression of the Laws of the Kingdom, and just Liberty of your People. For the taking away such Oppressions in Religion, church Government, and Discipline, as have been brought in and fomented by them. For uniting all such your Loyal Subjects together, as join in the same Fundamental Truths against the Papists, by removing some Oppressions and unnecessary Ceremonies, by which divers weak Consciences have been scrupled, and seem to be divided from the rest, and for the due Execution of those good Laws, which have been made for securing the Liberty of your Subjects.*[32]

Although Laud was never name-checked in the remonstrance, there was no need to identify him, everybody knew who was being blamed. Laud uttered a last prayer for Earl Strafford at his execution for treason at Tower Hill in May 1641 and afterwards remained a prisoner in the Tower until 1644.[33] However, this quiet spell of imprisonment did not last. The discovery of the king's plan to introduce his Irish army into the civil war being fought in England rekindled memories of Earl Strafford's impeachment just three years earlier. The names of Strafford and Laud as the enforcers of the king's policies in the 1630s went together like bread and butter as article seventy-six of the grand remonstrance makes clear:

> *76. The Parliament met upon the 13th of April 1640. The Earl of Strafford and Archbishop of Canterbury, with their Party, so prevailed with his Majesty, that the House of Commons was pressed to yield a Supply for Maintenance of the War with Scotland, before they had provided any Relief for the great and pressing Grievances of the People, which being against the fundamental Privilege and Proceeding of Parliament, was yet in humble Respect to his Majesty, so far admitted as that they agreed to take the matter of Supply into Consideration, and two several Days it was debated.*[34]

Bust of John Milton. Author's own used with kind permission of Master and Fellows of Christ's College Cambridge.

Bust of Robert Devereux, Third Earl of Essex. The Devereux home, just off the Strand, is now 'The Devereux' public house. Author's own.

Bust of Charles I. Author's own, used with kind permission of the Master and Wardens of the Worshipful Society of Apothecaries.

A young John Milton, painter and date unknown (public domain).

Bust of Oliver Cromwell, who famously rose from military commander during the civil wars to Lord Protector.

Sketch of Oliver Cromwell c/o Jane Young.

Devereux Arms oblique angle. Author's own

Sir Christopher Wren. Wren rebuilt London after the Great Fire of London in 1666.

William Prynne by
Wenceslas Hollar.
Prynne was a leading
light in the Leveller
movement. Believed to
be public domain.

Puritan preacher Richard
Baxter by Jonathan Spilsbury
(1763) after John Riley
(public domain).

Plaque commemorating the church of St John Zachery, destroyed in 1666.

Statue of Queen Elizabeth I at St Dunstan-in-the-West, Fleet Street. The sorry condition of the statue echoes the breakdown of the Elizabethan constitution under James I.

Pikemen of the Honourable Artillery Company, who provide the guard of honour for the Lord Mayor.

Shakespeare's Globe, Southwark. James I patronised the arts and Shakespeare's acting troupe became known as the 'King's Men'.

Section of the old Roman Wall, with later enhancements. During the civil war, this formed the inner ring of defence for the City.

Stock shot of civil war pikemen, a common sight during the civil war years.

Goldsmiths' Leopard, the symbol of the Goldsmiths.

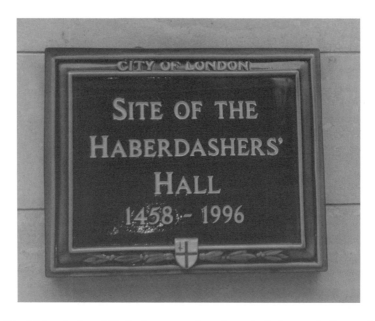

The Haberdashers' Hall plaque marks where their former hall stood.

Relief map of the Lines of Communication commissioned by Spitalfields Public Art 2007/8. Assigned to public domain.

Samuel Pepys. Pepys had parliamentarian connections through his family but became a royalist at the Restoration.

Demolition of the Cheapside Cross by Jane Young. Based on a near-contemporaneous engraving of the event.

Civil war skirmishers.

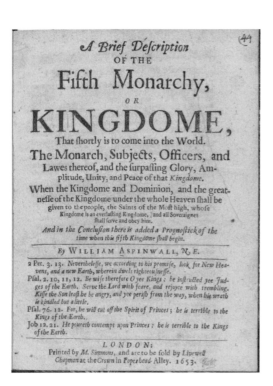

Fifth Monarchy Men tract by Richard Aspinall, 1653. Believed to be public domain.

Drilling the Militia by Alan Tucker.

Ironmonger Lane leading from Gresham Street to Cheapside.

St Olave Jewry, Ironmonger Lane. The Cromwellian government actively encouraged Jews to resettle in England during the 1650s.

Guildhall from Gresham Street. The sandy coloured parts are the original fifteenth century walls by John Croxton, the white portico was added in the eighteenth century by George Dance the Younger.

Plaque of the Irish Office. This was where the affairs of the Ulster Plantation were managed. Nowadays it is the offices of the City of London's Open Spaces Department.

Stationers' Hall. The Stationers' were tasked with enforcing copyright and censorship during the civil war years.

Nave of Christchurch Greyfriars. Burnt down in 1666 and rebuilt. Bombed out in the Blitz and now a public park.

Cutlers' Hall crest. The Cutlers' supplied the London Regiments with swords and belts.

Queen Anne by WF Bird. Anne was the last of the Stuart monarchs but finally achieved their long-cherished dream of uniting England and Scotland into Great Britain in 1707.

Paternoster by Elizabeth Frink in Paternoster Square.

City of London shield outside Goldsmiths' Hall. The Goldsmiths' hosted the Committee for Compounding Delinquents during the civil war years.

Temple Bar, rebuilt in 2005 and relocated in Paternoster Square.

The new Paul's Cross, rebuilt after the Second World War.

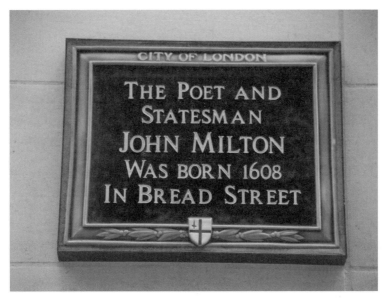

Plaque commemorating the birth of John Milton in 1608. Milton spoke six languages and became Cromwell's Secretary of Foreign Tongues in the 1650s.

Mercers' Maiden. The symbol of the Worshipful Company of Mercers.

Guildhall Yard, showing, the modern-day offices, the Aldermans' Court and Guildhall.

Section of London wall, by Salters' Hall.

William Shakespeare our greatest playwright. What dramas might he have written about the civil wars?

Wax Chandlers' Crest. Wax Chandlers manufactured relatively expensive wax candles.

Site of the Haberdashers' Hall in Gresham Street, now occupied by Lloyds Bank.

Isaac Pennington. MP for the City of London and Lord Mayor 1642-43. c/o Jane Young.

General George Monck. Royalist, turned parliamentarian, Cromwellian, then back to royalist at the restoration. c/o Jane Young.

Temple Bar, showing the royal crest. Until the 1870s, Temple Bar was part of the boundary between the City and Westminster.

Christchurch Greyfriars, choir.
Officers of the New Model Army
worshipped here in 1649 and
puritan preacher Richard Baxter
was buried here.

City Dragon by Alan Tucker.
The Dragon is the symbol of
the City of London.

By his association with Strafford, Laud was implicated in his downfall and the disgrace of Strafford eventually helped to condemn Laud. Laud's greatest enemy was the puritan William Prynne, whom Laud had prosecuted and maimed in the 1630s. Now Laud was imprisoned, Prynne took his revenge and repeatedly searched Laud's cell in the Tower for incriminating documents.[35] Laud's trial in the House of Lords on charges of treason and subverting the Protestant religion rumbled on through 1644, thanks to the mountain of evidence collected and presented by William Prynne.[36] Laud's trial was also uncannily similar to that of Strafford's just three years earlier. Despite the volume of evidence presented, or maybe because of it, the prosecutors were unable to secure a conviction. The Commons lost patience and on 31 October 1644 prepared an Act of Attainder against Laud, which was presented to the Lords on 22 November that year.[37] The Lords prevaricated but after much legal due process the ordinance was passed without amendment on 17 December. Laud was convicted:

> [...] for endeavouring to subvert the fundamental Laws and Government
> of the Kingdom of England, and, instead thereof, to introduce an arbitrary
> and tyrannical Government, against Law; and to alter and subvert God's
> true Religion by Law established in this Realm, and instead thereof to set up
> Popish Superstition and Idolatry; and to subvert the Rights of Parliaments,
> and the ancient Course of Parliamentary Proceedings; and, by false and
> malicious Slanders, to incense His Majesty against Parliaments; for which
> the Archbishop deserves to undergo the Pains and Forfeitures of High
> Treason; which said Offences have been sufficiently proved against the said
> Archbishop upon his Impeachment: Be it therefore Ordered and Ordained,
> by the Lords and Commons in this present Parliament assembled, and by
> Authority of the same, That he said Archbishop, for the Offences aforesaid,
> stand and be adjudged attainted of High Treason, and shall suffer the Pains
> of Death, and shall incur all Forfeitures both of Lands and Goods, as a
> Person attainted of High Treason should or ought to do.[38]

Laud's trial and execution on January 1645 was the eventual outcome of just one of many great matters that occupied the Lords and Commons that autumn, which may account for its slow progress through the upper chamber. Negotiations with the king had been carrying on through 1644 and, as Gardiner notes, this may have made some of the Lords hesitate before proceeding against the king's appointment to the highest clerical office in the kingdom.[39] The other great matter was reform of the parliamentarian war effort, via the Self-Denying Ordinance. Members of the Commons and Lords would be required to relinquish their political status to retain their military commands. As Ian Gentles notes, the majority of peers were opposed to this because whereas MPs could resign their seats, peers could not.[40] Although the Self-Denying Ordinance was initially rejected, it was eventually passed by the Lords in April 1645.[41]

What was the essence of charges against Laud? One of the charges was that Laud had attempted to 'subvert God's true religion' and 'set up Popish Superstition and Idolatry'.[42] The 'Popish superstition' in and outside of churches has been discussed. Laud's other major offence, in the eyes of his accusers, was that he innovated forms of worship. The attempted introduction of the *Book of Common Prayer* in Scotland was a case in point, because the crown's inept response to its rejection by the Scottish church caused the bishops' wars and indirectly led to the wars of three kingdoms.[43] However, it would have been a more accurate charge to say that Laud had reverted, rather than innovated, worship back towards Roman Catholicism. The re-establishment of Episcopacy and insistence on worshipping according to the *Book of Common Prayer* were but steps on that backward journey towards papacy.[44] In the eyes of puritans, that was Laud's real offence.

How did these religious reforms, the ordering of acts of iconoclasm and the removal of Archbishop Laud and his innovations, translate into everyday life at parish level? How did churches in the city react to the orders issued in September 1641? An analysis carried out by Julie Spraggon indicates that of twenty-nine parishes surveyed, eighteen complied with the orders by removing images and fifteen removed communion rails or moved altar tables.[45] Although this is an incomplete survey from over a hundred city parishes, due to gaps in the parish records, they yield certain conclusions, if this sample is representative. The removal of ungodly images and rails and moving communion tables and altars back to their original positions before Laud's reforms indicate these were somewhat higher priorities over levelling of chancels, the removal or defacing of inscriptions, crosses or organs.[46] As Dr Spraggon notes, some of the iconoclastic actions may have anticipated the orders issued on 8 September, while some parishes were slow to comply with them. Remarkably, these include St Lawrence Jewry, which sat opposite Guildhall, where the removal of rails was delayed until June 1642 and St Dionis Backchurch, which levelled its chancel in the year before Easter 1643, just a few days before the Harley Committee was formed.[47] The Harley Committee was, therefore, not starting a new venture, but picking up and continuing an existing exercise on a more formalised basis.

Dr Spraggon's analysis of the responses to the Harley Committee and the ordinance of August 1643 indicates a slight widening of priorities. Whereas the parishes that complied with the orders of September 1641 focused on removal of communion rails and images, the reported response to the ordinances issued in 1643 indicates that iconoclasm was directed at a broader spectrum of church furniture and fittings. Of the thirty-six parishes analysed by Dr Spraggon, fourteen reported removal or defacement of images, but twenty parishes also reported the removal of steeples and similar crosses, and thirteen removed or defaced inscriptions.[48] The parishes of Allhallows Barking and St Lawrence Jewry reported they had removed their communion rails and images by 1642. However, both parishes reported further action to remove or deface images in 1643/44. This may indicate several possibilities. The Harley Committee may have been dissatisfied with progress in complying with the 1641 orders and insisted on a further wave of iconoclasm within these parishes, or that the task of identifying and destroying ungodly images was so big an undertaking it was reported twice. What can we learn from this? Remembering the caveat about this being an incomplete survey, any projection of the sample as representative of the whole is informed speculation. However, as Dr Spraggon notes, there is secondary evidence in the form of petitions to the long parliament to support these conclusions from the available data.[49]

One of the most radical parishes in the city during the civil war and afterwards was the now defunct St Stephen Coleman Street, just two streets away from the Guildhall. Its minister was John Goodwin, who was born in Norfolk in 1594 and matriculated from Queen's College Cambridge with an MA in 1617. Goodwin married and, taking holy orders, arrived in London in 1632. Bishop Juxon appointed Goodwin to the living of St Stephen in 1633, when his predecessor John Davenport was ejected after joining the dissenters.[50] The parish was evidently already on its way to becoming a centre of puritanism within the city. If Bishop Juxon hoped that Goodwin would be a calming influence and docilely lead his flock, he was mistaken. Goodwin followed his predecessor's example in taking the dissenting puritan viewpoint. On several occasions in the 1630s, Goodwin was called before Bishop Juxon to explain or apologise for his words or deeds. Juxon was a quiet, tolerant bishop who evidently believed in managing not confronting his ministers. Although he supported Archbishop Laud and assisted him, with misgivings, in writing the Scots prayer book, Juxon may be described as a moderate churchman. However, Juxon's choice of minister at St Stephen would prove to be anything but moderate.

During the civil war years from 1642 to 1645, Goodwin's radicalism increased. Regrettably, there is no information available as to the extent St Stephen Coleman Street co-operated with either the orders of 8 September 1641 or the Harley Committee. However, given what we know of the character of its minister, it is unlikely that Laudian innovations were allowed to remain. In 1645, however, Goodwin himself was removed from St Stephen because he only offered baptism and holy communion to a select few of his parishioners. The favoured few were chosen by a committee consisting of himself, his wife and thirteen others. Goodwin promptly set-up an independent church in the same parish. In 1647, the parishioners of St Stephen petitioned parliament that Goodwin be appointed to preach 'every Lord's Day', which effectively meant Goodwin was the *de facto* preacher in residence, and in 1649 he was officially restored to the living, replacing William Taylor. Goodwin's radical puritan outlook must have agreed with the new regime that emerged after Pride's Purge. He expressed approval at the purge and, although he visited the king between his trial and execution, satisfied himself that the trial and sentence of the king was legal.[51]

Goodwin appears to have been tolerated by the Commonwealth, especially after his service of thanksgiving after the Battle of Worcester in 1651. He was impressed with the work of John Milton and cited his writings in his pamphlets and sermons. However, Goodwin and controversy were never far away and in the 1650s his writings delighted and offended in equal measure, including an ill-advised attack on the Commission of Triers that had been established in 1654 to inspect ministers in their parishes. The 'Triers' were supported by 'Ejectors' who expelled unsuitable ministers and schoolmasters, a process that Goodwin was familiar with. Predictably, in 1657 he was removed from the parish. At the restoration, Goodwin and Milton were arrested. Milton was tried as a republican and an advocate of regicide and could have been condemned to death, but the sentence was commuted due to his blindness.[52] Goodwin displayed good sense and he eventually received his freedom, but joined the group of eighteen persons forever barred from holding public office under the Act of Free and General Pardon, Indemnity and Oblivion.[53] Later, he returned to his old parish in Coleman Street until his death in September 1665.

One last controversy connected with the parish remains, the story of the Fifth Monarchy Men. These were extreme puritans who were active during the 1650s, otherwise known as the interregnum. Based on muddled interpretations of the books of Daniel and Revelations in the bible, they believed that four great epochs in history, Babylonian, Persian, Greek and Roman, would be succeeded by the Fifth Monarchy, when Christ reigned for 1,000 years until judgement day.[54] One of the effects of the civil war was to break up the monopoly of religious thought imposed by the Anglican church so that, within the wider sphere of Christianity, religious sects and cults flourished.[55] The roots of this went back to the Reformation when the emphasis on private prayer and reading the bible without necessarily requiring the intermediary presence of a priest to explain its meaning, enabled worshippers to have a personal relationship with God. In addition, the tumultuous events of the civil wars prompted millennial fears that the second coming of Christ was approaching. Thus, religious groups emerged, such as Quakers, Fifth Monarchists, Muggletonians and Ranters, to name just four of the better known. Two of these movements began in London during the interregnum. The Muggletonians were formed in 1651 when two merchant tailors, Lodowicke Muggleton and John Reeve, heard the call of God and announced they were the prophets mentioned in the Book of Revelations. Their movement spurned intellectual reason as everything that happened had an explanation in the bible. They were opposed to the Quakers because they didn't believe in evangelising, nor did they worship on the premise that God was uninterested in events on earth. However, they did believe that Christ would affect a second coming.[56]

The Fifth Monarchy Men were similarly formed in London by members of the church congregation of Allhallows-the-Great, off Thames Street.[57] They were impatient with the purged parliament for dragging its feet on religious reform, something that was also a growing worry for Oliver Cromwell. Although Cromwell politically and religiously was an independent, he was in contact with men like Major-General Thomas Harrison, who was a republican and Fifth Monarchist.[58] As the movement grew and spread, it found fertile ground in other puritan centres in the city, such as St Stephen Coleman Street. Its sometime minister, John Goodwin, had written tracts denouncing the movement in 1654 and 1655.[59] Yet the relationship between the parish and the Fifth Monarchists is ambiguous. After Thomas Venner's failed uprising of the Fifth Monarchy Men in 1661, the members of the parish protested their innocence and disclaimed any knowledge or involvement. Yet the plot was hatched in Coleman Street and at least one source states the conspirators met in the minister's study. Venner's plot failed and he and the ringleaders were executed.[60] In the long run, the only achievement of the Fifth Monarchists was to instil mistrust between non-conformists and high churchmen and their royal master, the restored King Charles II. Ultimately, this would lead to strict sanctions against non-conformists preaching or holding civic offices in London.[61]

On the other hand, there were men who were puritan but were prepared to acknowledge and accept a broad church. Richard Baxter was a puritan from Kidderminster who was drawn into the war as chaplain to Colonel Whalley's Regiment of Horse.[62] Baxter preached the Protestant ethos of justification by faith alone, but almost as a concession advocated that faith must be accompanied by at least an element of repentance of sin and asking God's forgiveness. This last was a muddled theological position and a bold statement.[63] Baxter's religious positioning was, therefore, halfway between Calvinism and Arminianism. During the commonwealth, Baxter preached against Oliver Cromwell's government and was summoned to explain himself. He was interviewed by Oliver Cromwell and the two men enjoyed a frank exchange of religious views without fear or favour, something of a rarity in this period. In retrospect, we can see that Baxter was neither a die-hard puritan nor an anti-monarchist. Baxter had a second interview with Oliver Cromwell and gave his opinions of the liberty of tender conscience, which evidently chimed with Cromwell's ideas. Baxter's, and later Cromwell's, model of the liberty of tender conscience meant freedom of worship, for all except Roman Catholics.[64]

In this all too brief survey of religious strife in London and the kingdoms during the civil war years and before, several themes have emerged. Religious conflict underpinned and fuelled the civil war, far more than arguments about the state of the economy, as it was understood, for example. The Elizabethan church settlement was more or less copied by James: mainstream Protestantism with bishops, and, initially, quiet toleration of Roman Catholics and puritans. Once these groups started to make trouble, however, for instance after the Gunpowder Plot, the velvet gloves came off. James' religious policy, intentionally or not, mirrored that of Elizabeth and, like Elizabeth's, his religious settlement just about survived to the end of his reign. However, this fragile house of cards tottered during Charles' reign. His clumsy attempts to synchronise the mode of worship throughout his kingdoms and return it to his ideal high church model fragmented his kingdoms, leading to civil war. The puritan backlash could not be contained, and at the end of the conflict, the dismantling of the Anglican near-monopoly of worship provided the seed-bed for many breakaway religious groups. The physical and political structure of London, with its small parishes, alehouses and livery companies, where worshippers of a like mind could meet in private, provided the fertiliser for religious splinter groups, cults and sects. This posed a massively complicated question for the Commonwealth and its successors in the restoration and beyond: is it humanly possible to have a national, unified church and respect freedom of worship, liberty of tender conscience?

Chapter 6

Publish what you like?

The wars of three kingdoms were wars of politics and wars of religion. The first of these assertions is a given, since by their nature civil wars are the ultimate expression of a political crisis. The second assertion is an accurate description. Unsightly strands of religious discord run through the history of the civil wars, like a series of mismatched threads in a tapestry. However, the civil wars in the three kingdoms may claim another descriptor: the war of public opinion. The civil wars were a conflict fought not only with sword, pike and musket. There was a fourth weapon to hand that was intangible, ever-present, and just as deadly as a sword thrust or musket ball. Public opinion. This has, of course, existed since humans started to think and communicate. Until the advent of print, however, public opinion could only be propagated orally, or written by hand. Documents could only be laboriously copied by hand, which slowed the rate of publication and also aided the authorities in identifying the author, as their handwriting would be recognisable. The invention of the printing press, with its revolutionary movable letters, by Gutenberg in the mid-fifteenth century, was a game-changer. A printer could now produce as many copies of a book in a day that written by hand might take a week to transcribe. The introduction of the printing press to England, by William Caxton, presented the authorities with a serious headache. Not everything written was complimentary about the church or the government.

Just off Ludgate Hill is a small alleyway that leads to the hall of one of the most important livery companies in the city, and one very much involved in the civil war. The Worshipful Company of Stationers was formed in 1403. They were booksellers who populated the area around St Paul's Cathedral. Each bookseller had his 'station' or place where he sold his books and the name stuck, hence 'stationers'. The company was created just as written books started to be overtaken by printed books. However, the stationers were forward-thinking and instead of attempting to block the new technology they embraced it.[1] In 1557, they received their royal charter from Mary I. This was a milestone in their history. The charter not only recognised the stationers as a livery company, it also awarded them the monopoly of printing in London with rights of search for illegal books, those printed without being registered at Stationers' Hall or smuggled into the country. Every book published was required to be registered at Stationers' Hall. The printer would have to establish his 'copy-right', in other words he had the right, given by the author, of printing copies. Hence, the term 'copyright' evolved. Nowadays, of course, copyright automatically belongs to the owner of the work in question. In the sixteenth and seventeenth centuries, copyright was a legal protection to printers. The change in awarding copyright to authors came in 1710 by a statute passed under Queen Anne.[2]

The enforcement of copyright went hand-in-hand with censorship. The growth of printing was the information superhighway of the early modern period. Books, pamphlets, tracts, sermons and newsbooks were now relatively cheaply and widely available to those who could read. Newspapers in their modern form didn't appear until the eighteenth century. *The Daily Courant*, London's first newspaper, was first published in 1702. A considerable proportion of the population in London and elsewhere were literate.[3] Members of the church and sons of the gentry, and educated merchants, journeymen and apprentices, were literate and numerate. Going down the social scale, literacy rates obviously varied. But there was another factor in play that influenced the literacy of working men and women. The Reformation of the sixteenth century introduced a new model of worship that encouraged people to enter into a personal relationship with God. Worshippers still attended churches, albeit somewhat stripped of their ornamentation, and said their prayers. However, the Reformation also placed greater emphasis on reading the bible and thinking about its message. Previously worshippers attended mass, heard an extract from the bible, in Latin of course, and their priest explained it. Now they attended sermons in church and devout worshippers might take notes. Regularly reading the bible in English improved literacy rates.

There was another unexpected side effect. Thinking about the bible and its messages meant that, slowly, hesitantly, working men and women started to think for themselves. The idea that ordinary people might engage in, literally, critical analysis of the church or government policy did not sit well with their superiors on the social scale. There is an old saying, 'cobbler, stick to thy last', which is taken to mean working people should concentrate on their profession and not get above themselves. The phrase may have originated in an anecdote of Greek philosopher Pliny, who related the story of the artist Appelles of Kos, who displayed his pictures and invited passers-by to critique them. When a cobbler criticised Apelles' drawing of a sandal, the artist corrected the image. However, when the cobbler began appraising the depiction of the subject's leg, Apelles is said to have retorted '*Ne supra trepipam suitor*', 'let the shoemaker venture no further'.[4] In the context of the civil war years, when ordinary men and women not only stepped out of their usual spheres of existence, but, like the cobbler in the anecdote, challenged the structure of the political body in the three kingdoms, this resonates.

However, the authorities were not going to accept the widespread publication of books without imposing a degree of regulation, and the stationers' company was responsible for identifying and prosecuting printers of offensive books that were critical of government or church, or merely posing and exploring ideas that the common man had no business thinking about. Cyprian Blagden notes that the stationers' ambition to form a great trading empire neatly coincided with the contract as the official censor of the English government.[5] Penalties for infractions could be severe. In 1631, the royal printers Robert Barker and Martin Lucas were fined £3,000 and had their printing licence rescinded. Their offence was to publish a work without correcting a simple typographic error. Barker and Lucas's edition of the *King James Bible* omitted the single word 'not' from the Book of Exodus, Chapter 20, Verse 14. The seventh commandment thus read 'Thou shalt commit adultery'. This was scandalous and the offending copies, now dubbed the 'wicked bible' were ordered to be burnt.[6] The company was also not afraid to flex its muscles in its own interest. In 1635, the stationers referred their long-running dispute with the booksellers to Archbishop Laud. Their appeal was successful and, in 1635, the stationers obtained a favourable ruling from the star chamber that imposed a ban on unbound books being sent out of London, except the two universities, which were considered special cases.[7] This was a case of the company defending its monopoly in London and beyond. Bookbinding was another aspect of the stationers' business, as was illustrating, practised by the Limners. The Bookbinders and Limners Companies were formerly independent, but were absorbed by the stationers so they controlled the entire process of producing books. Monopoly of trade meant just that.

However, the stationers' good fortune suffered in the early 1640s. Charles' constitutional experiment of divine rule ended when he was forced to recall parliament in 1640. As previously discussed, the short parliament called in the spring of 1640 failed to achieve anything. However, the parliament called in November 1640 was more durable and its members wiser and more tenacious in their opposition to the king than its predecessor. The long parliament focused on reigning-in the king's powers, rather than trying to resurrect a debate on royal government in the 1630s. One of the first casualties of the long parliament's new political agenda was the reviled star chamber, which was finally abolished on 5 July 1641.[8] This was a blow to the stationers, who depended on the star chamber as both threat and ultimate sanction.[9] During the civil war years, the stationers' experience roughly mirrors the progress of the war. From autumn 1640 to late summer 1642, there was still just about a central government in the three kingdoms, although from January 1642 it was increasingly strained and divided. From November 1640 to January 1642, at least there was a king in parliament. From January 1642, there was a reduced parliament, and from 1644, there were two parliaments – what remained of the old parliament in London, and the royalist parliament in Oxford. Between 1642 and 1646, therefore, there was a gradual weakening of the grip of central government. This resulted in a proliferation of newsbooks and pamphlets. For a short while, it was almost a case of publish what you like.

In the uncertain period between the king summoning parliament in November 1640 and his undignified flight from London in January 1642, both king and parliament had more important and urgent matters to think about apart from censorship. There was a time when the controlling hand of state relaxed its grip somewhat. Of course, the strength of that grip has been disputed.[10] The Stationers' Company could not regulate publications not passed for inspection at Stationers' Hall, nor those smuggled in from abroad. And in the early years of the civil wars, that grip loosened even further. Rival newsbooks, the ancestors of modern day newspapers, began to appear, at first quietly and surreptitiously, then openly. Their titles indicate their allegiance: *Mercurius Aulicus: A Diurnal Communicating the Intelligence and Affaires of the Court to the Rest of the Kingdom* was one of the first royalist newsbooks. It was published in Oxford, which was the king's adopted capital from 1642 to 1646. As a city, Oxford was not dissimilar to London in that allegiance in the general population was split between king and parliament. Although Oxford was known as the king's unofficial capital, the colleges that were part of the university were royalist, whereas the town was pro-parliamentarian.[11] For a short period, however, until the king's forces marched in after Edgehill, Oxford was an open city where royalist and parliamentarian mingled, although not always peacefully:

Parliamentary troops moved in and out of Oxford until mid-October, not always peacefully: some mutinied at a muster in the Parks and drunken rival factions fought at Carfax. A company of London dragoneers went armed to church because of the enmity of the town and scholars, and when the mayoral elections were held on 19 September the city rejected Lord Say's candidate, John Nixon, because of his earlier flight to Abingdon, and elected Thomas Dennis.[12]

Mercurius Aulicus was published between 1643 and 1645 to counter the sea of propaganda pouring out of parliamentarian-held London. Of course, anybody found selling royalist newsbooks in parliamentarian-held towns and cities, like London, was likely to be arrested. Royalist newsbooks were mainly printed in Oxford, utilising the university printing press, although a handful were secretly printed in London.[13] Those printed in Oxford were smuggled into the city and sold by married women who concealed them and covert messages in their underskirts.[14] Respectable married women were considered unlikely to be searched for illicit materials and the women had a legal defence. Even if they were caught red-handed, they could plead marital coercion and obedience to the will of their husbands. As such, the weight of the law would fall upon the husband. The issue of an arrest warrant for inciting others to take arms against parliament was a simple process. On the other hand, if the husband was serving in the king's army somewhere between London and Bristol or York, for example, the execution of the arrest warrant was a different matter altogether.

Parliamentarians published newsbooks, of course, with titles such as *The Parliament Hawk*, whose title told its readers it was keeping watch over the kingdom, and *Parliament's Spie* (*sic*), which similarly implied it was ferreting out stories the royalists would rather keep secret. *Mercurius Aulicus* alone references nine parliamentarian newsbooks.[15] Both royalist and parliamentarian newsbooks adopted an editorial style somewhat similar to modern-day tabloid newspapers. Glaring headlines proclaimed great victories, or decrying complaints when describing a defeat or setback. There was precious little middle-of-the-road fact-checked impartial reporting. A handful of hard facts were wrapped up in a cloud of emotionally charged propaganda. Emotive language such as 'outrage' and 'murder' featured prominently. Events were rarely recorded contemporaneously, and when finally published could be anything from a few hours old to several months and would be liable to inconsistencies, received memories and outright embroidery. One notable example is the royalist churchman Bruno Ryves who, in June 1643, started publishing his short-lived *Mercurius Rusticus; or the Countries Complaint of the Barbarous Outrages committed by the Sectaries of this late flourishing Kingdom*, which ran for nineteen editions until December 1643.[16] Ryve's first edition of *Mercurius Rusticus* gave an account of the Colchester riots that took place in August 1642, when the townsfolk of Colchester rioted after arresting the royalist Sir John Lucas on the point of his departure to liaise with the king at Nottingham.[17] Ryve's earlier editions of his *Mercurius* focused on describing the brutality of parliamentarian soldiers and their supporters, while later editions lamented the wave of iconoclasm that was directed against the cathedrals.[18]

One notable Londoner who temporarily became a publisher was the wood-turner Nehemiah Wallington. Wallington was born in the parish of St Leonard Eastcheap in 1598 and followed his father's trade and faith as a puritan. He set up his own shop in Eastcheap in 1620, but his puritan outlook and passion for collecting books got him into hot water, when he was presented before the star chamber to explain his possession of books like William Prynne's *Divine Tragedy* and Henry Burton's *Apology of an Appeal*. Wallington escaped sanction when he admitted his past ownership of the books but claimed to have disposed of them some time before the inquiry in the star chamber. In this, Wallington was more fortunate than the authors of these prohibited tracts. Prynne had his ears cropped, was pilloried and fined. Burton was similarly ear-cropped and later both men were sent to prison. Wallington published three main works in his lifetime. In 1630, he started compiling his *Historical Notes and Meditations, 1583-1649*, which Wallington created by compiling cuttings of tracts, embellishing them with commentary based on tittle-tattle, which lent a sense of gravitas with a leavening of his virtuous thoughts, hence the 'Meditations'. Wallington also maintained his *Journals*, which narrated, rather more accurately, his private life. A third volume, partly an edited series of excerpts from his *Historical Notes*, augmented with observations of strange phenomena, attributed to God's wrath on 'Sabbath breakers and Drunkards'. Regrettably, we know nothing about Wallington's thoughts on events in the 1650s because his *Historical Notes* ends after his account of the execution of the king. Wallington died in late 1658, the same year as Oliver Cromwell, and was thus spared the disappointment of seeing the fall of the godly republic he believed in.[19]

While Nehemiah Wallington escaped serious censure for owning books written by Prynne and Bastwick, those particular authors were less fortunate. William Prynne was born in 1600 and his early life marked him for the professions involving paper and ink. He attended Bath Grammar School, Oriel College Oxford, Lincolns Inn, and was called to the Bar in 1628. However, his love of the law was conflated with a strong religious bent. In 1624, Prynne began writing what would become a 1,000-page criticism of stage plays as immoral, published in 1632 under the title *Histriomastix*. This was taken as a libel against Queen Henrietta Maria, who enjoyed amateur dramatics, and Prynne soon experienced the law from the perspective of the accused. A year's imprisonment in the Tower was followed by a £5,000 fine, the revocation of his degree and the loss of his ears.[20] His companion in travail, John Bastwick, was similarly fined, ear-cropped and sentenced to life imprisonment. Bastwick was originally held in the Tower. However, the authorities must have feared they were creating a martyr and he was transferred to St Mary's Castle on the Isle of Scilly.[21] In 1640, Prynne and Bastwick were released by parliament and entered London as heroes.[22] Bastwick later took a military commission and served as captain in the Leicester Regiments. On being captured by royalists, he was briefly imprisoned and soon after continued his writings.[23] One of Bastwick's friends at this time was the political agitator John Lilburne.

Lilburne was an adoptive Londoner, born at Greenwich in about 1614. The exact date of Lilburne's birth is unclear and Lilburne himself often muddied the waters about his true age. He was apprenticed with Thomas Hewson, a London cloth wholesaler, from 1630 to 1636, which would have made him 16 when he began his apprenticeship.[24] In 1636, Lilburne fell in with John Bastwick and William Prynne. He was closely connected with these two, helping to print and sell Prynne's *News from Ipswich*, an action that got him arrested and presented before the star chamber. Lilburne stood his ground, refusing to incriminate himself, and he challenged the court's authority. His stance forced the star chamber to pass a decree prohibiting works to be printed before being inspected:

> *That none shall presume to Print any Book or Pamphlet whatsoever, unless the same be first Licensed with all the Titles, Epistles, and Prefaces therewith imprinted, by the Lord Arch-bishop of Canterbury, or the Bishop of London for the time being, or by their appointment; and within the Limits of either University, by the Chancellor or Vice-Chancellor thereof.*[25]

The ordinance concludes by describing the punishment that was meted out to Lilburne:

> *And that if any Person whatsoever that is not an allowed Printer shall presume to set up a Press for Printing, or work at any such Press, or Set and*

Compose Letters for the same, he shall be set in the Pillory, and whipped
through the City of London.[26]

The star chamber judges sentenced Lilburne to be pilloried, fined £500 and whipped from the River Fleet to Palace Yard. Lilburne, however, remained unbroken during his ordeal and called out to the spectators to this bizarre ritual, denouncing bishops and distributing copies of Bastwick's writings. Eventually, the authorities realised this punishment was counter-productive. Instead of deterring similar behaviour it was drawing attention to it and Lilburne was silenced with a gag and removed from the scene.[27] Lilburne was released by the long parliament in 1640 and, on 5 May 1641, the Commons voted that the sentence of the star chamber in 1637 was not only illegal, it was 'bloody, wicked, cruel, barbarous, and tyrannical'.[28]

When the civil wars broke out, Lilburne took a commission as captain in Lord Brooke's regiment, fighting at Edgehill and Brentford. Captured at Brentford, he was taken to Oxford and charged with treason, coming close to being executed. However, news of his capture and court-martial reached parliament who, in December 1642, told the king, in no uncertain terms, that if Lilburne and other captured parliamentarian soldiers were executed, the king's men held by parliament could expect to suffer the same fate.[29] The war rumbled on and Lilburne rose to lieutenant-colonel, but found he could not take the solemn league and covenant, and resigned his commission in April 1645.[30] The soldier's career was over, that of the political agitator just about to begin. Lilburne was implicated in the argument between the Earl of Manchester, who he disliked, and Cromwell, who had supported Lilburne when he asked parliament to overturn his sentence in 1641. Lilburne went too far, however, and opined that in advocating peace with the king, Manchester was guilty of treason. This was too much and Lilburne was summoned before the Lords. During this inquiry, Lilburne repeated the blocking tactics he had used against the star chamber. The outcome was predictable, Lilburne was fined £4,000, imprisoned in the Tower and disqualified from accepting a civil or military position for life.[31]

While the removal of restrictions on printing was welcome to those who wished to attack the king's policies and those of his evil advisers, others realised the dangers. Firstly, the benefit of a free press cuts both ways. Pro-parliamentarian newsbooks attacking the king could be countered by pro-royalist propaganda. In 1641, parliament had established their Committee for Printing. Now, two years later, the markets in London and everywhere else were being flooded with competing newsbooks: the *Parliament Spy* and

Parliament Kite on one side and various incarnations of the royalist newsbook *Mercurius*. On the other News was rarely current, royalist Bruno Ryve's account of the riots in Colchester in August 1642 was published nearly a year later. Accuracy of fact was a luxury. In spring 1643, Henry Parker, then secretary to the parliamentarian army, later secretary to the House of Commons, drafted a 'humble remonstrance' on behalf of the stationers. The eventual response from parliament was to issue an ordinance regulating printing. The introduction states:

> *I Imprimis, That no Person or Persons whatsoever shall presume to Print or cause to be Printed, either in the Parts beyond the Seas, or in this Realm, or other his Majesty's Dominions, any Seditious, Schismatic, or offensive Books or Pamphlets, to the scandal of Religion, or the church, or the Government, or Governors of the church and State, or Common-wealth, or of any corporation, or particular Person or Persons whatsoever, nor shall import any such Book or Books, nor sell or dispose of them, or any of them, nor cause any such to be Bound, Stitched, or Sowed, upon Pain of he or they so offending, shall lose all such Books and Pamphlets, and also have, and sustain such Correction, and severe Punishment, either by Fine, Imprisonment, or other Corporal Punishment, or otherwise, as by this Court, or by his Majesty's Commissioners for Causes Ecclesiastical in the High Commission Court respectively as the several Causes shall require, shall be thought fit to be inflicted upon him, or them, for such their Offence and Contempt.*[32]

Note the reference to corporal punishment. William Prynne, John Bastwick and Henry Burton had been pilloried, flogged and had their ears cropped for writing libels against Archbishop Laud in the 1630s.[33] However, in 1640 these men were released by the long parliament and resumed their career. During the latter half of the civil war years, the flood of publications clearly demonstrated that the Ordinance for Regulating of Printing wasn't effective. Just as the split in Protestant worship between high and low church paved the way for the multitude of religious sects, so the relative weakness in government was reflected by its inability to regulate the flow of printed material. George Thomason, for example, made a point of collecting as many newsbooks and tracts as possible. He collected 2,134 in 1642 and, despite the ordinance, over the course of the 1640s amassed a library of 4,044 volumes.[34] Parliament attempted to control this deluge of print by issuing further ordinances regarding printing in 1647 and 1649. On 30

September 1647, parliament issued an 'Ordinance against unlicensed or scandalous Pamphlets'. This ordinance sought to stop the printing of illicit publications and generally regulate the print industry, an aim that benefitted the stationers as well as parliament. Significantly, the ordinance emphasised works printed and published in the 'Cities of London and Westminster'. In 1647, London had repositioned itself somewhat from its previous support of parliament and the New Model Army. The penalties were severe:

> *That is to say, The Maker, Writer or Composer of any such Unlicensed Book, Pamphlet, Treatise, Ballad, Libel, Sheet or sheets of News, shall forfeit and pay Forty shillings, or be Imprisoned in the Common Goal for the County or Liberty where the Offence is committed, or the Offender shall be found, until he shall pay the same, so that the said Imprisonment exceed not forty days; The Printer to forfeit and pay Twenty shillings, and suffer the like Imprisonment, until he pay the same, the said Imprisonment not exceeding Twenty days, and likewise to have his Press and Implements of Imprinting seized and broken in pieces; The Book-seller or Stationer to forfeit and pay ten shillings, or be Imprisoned in like manner until he pay the same, the Imprisonment not exceeding Ten days, And the Hawker, Peddler or Ballad-singer to forfeit and lose all his Books, Pamphlets and printed Papers exposed to sale, and also to be whipped as a Common Rogue, in the Liberty or Parish where the said Offender shall be apprehended, or the Offence committed*[35].

This ordinance adds that the penalties for writing, printing and selling unlicensed publications did not exempt the persons guilty of committing these offences from further sanctions if the writings in question were found to be 'Seditious, Treasonable, or Blasphemous matter'.[36] How effective was this ordinance? The evidence is circumstantial, but the fact that less than two years after the ordinance was issued, the parliament of the young republic issued a similar, but much more detailed, Act of Parliament regarding printing is an indicator. The 'Act against Unlicensed and Scandalous Books and Pamphlets, and for better regulating of Printing' was passed on 20 September 1649 and stated the following: publication of weekly pamphlets caused 'mischief' and laws against 'spreaders of false news' were to be enforced. The Act states, in part, that writers of seditious material were to be fined £10, the printer £5, and the seller £2. Purchasers of such material were given one day to disclose their knowledge of the publication to the lord mayor or equivalent authority, or be liable to a penalty of £1 per item thus concealed from the authorities. All licences for printing newsbooks were revoked and were to be reissued by the clerk of parliament. Printers were to submit bonds of £300, and were barred from taking houses or lodgings without first notifying the master and wardens of the Stationers' Company, on pain of incurring a fine of £5 per offence.[37] This Act clearly gives the Stationers' Company greater powers, including search and seizure, although the final responsibility for enforcement fell with the council of state.[38]

> *And be it further Enacted by the Authority aforesaid, That all former Licenses granted by Authority of both or either House of Parliament to any person or persons, for Printing any Diurnal, News or Occurrences, shall be from henceforth void and of no further effect; And that no Book, Pamphlet, sheet or sheets of News or Occurrences whatsoever, shall henceforth be printed, bound, stitched or put to sale by any person or persons whatsoever, unless the same be first approved of and Licensed under the hand of the Clerk of the Parliament, or of such person as shall be authorized by the Council of State for the time being; or (for so much as may concern the Affairs of the Army) under the hand of the Secretary of the Army for the time being, the same to be entered in their several Registers, to be by them kept for that purpose; and also in the Register-book of the Company of Stationers, according to ancient custom; and the Printer thereof to put his hand thereto.*[39]

Why would parliament and the Stationers' Company feel there was a need for this tougher regulation? We have already seen how the long parliament's toleration of weakened controls on printing, to enable criticism of the king's policies, partially failed, due to the law of unforeseen consequences. Sauce for the goose, as the old saying goes, is sauce for the gander. The re-imposition of government censorship after the civil wars was difficult, but not impossible. On the other hand, the removal in 1641 of the dreadful threat of being presented before the star chamber encouraged writers, printers and sellers. Another side-effect of the partial lapse in de-regulation during the civil war years was that printers could sell their wares direct to purchasers, thus cutting out the middle men, the booksellers.[40] From the stationers' point of view, this could not be allowed to happen. The printers were not overly discouraged at this clampdown, however, and in 1651, the printers unsuccessfully petitioned the Committee for the Better Regulating of Printing for the right to become a fraternity, or even a company independent of the stationers. In their petition, the printers cited the example of the

Worshipful Society of Apothecaries, who in 1617 had split from the grocers and formed their own company.[41]

This extract from the Act, above, yields a little more to analysis. Parliament as the originator of the Act is mentioned early, but it should be noted that the council of state and the army are referenced virtually in the same sentence. Significantly, the closing paragraph cites the requirement for names of publications and their authors to be entered into the 'Register-book of the Company of Stationers, according to ancient custom'. Those last four words were clearly intended to convey a sense of continuity, rather than ongoing revolution. The revolution is over, long live the commonwealth.

However, some thought the revolution, far from being over, had just began. John Lilburne, now popularly known as 'Free Born John' in reference to his dogged defence before the judges of the star chamber, was the figurehead of the movement known as Levellers that emerged during the uncertain peace of 1646–47. The Levellers were an offshoot of the breakdown in civic, religious and military discipline that occurred towards the end of the civil wars. It has been asserted that London was the breeding place of the Levellers. Its close-knit system of parishes, maze of streets with churches, alehouses and other meeting places, were fertile ground for the propagation of ideas.[42] The emergence of the Levellers and similar groups was a natural consequence of the conflict. To the grandees, the senior officers, of the New Model Army, however, the Levellers were a nuisance to be dealt with. Despite three different publications entitled *An Agreement of the People*, the third version of which John Lilburne co-wrote, and the famous Putney debates in 1647, where the army council debated in the church of St Mary's, Putney, the shape of any future settlement, this wasn't going to happen. *The Agreement of the People* broadly called for freedom of religion, an amnesty regarding involvement in the civil wars, an extension of voting rights to ordinary working men, and an election for parliament every two years.[43]

Although some of these demands, freedom of religion and a widened electoral franchise exist nowadays, in the mid-seventeenth century they were an aspiration for those asking, and an impertinent demand from those in power. In opposition to the *Agreement of the People*, the grandees published their *Heads of Proposals*. These were drafted by the astute solicitor Henry Ireton, and presented by him at the Putney debates. In essence, they were not so dissimilar to the propositions offered to the king in 1641 and again in 1643. Royalists were to be disbarred from position or office for five years. Parliament was to set a date for its dissolution and future parliaments called every two years. Parliament had the veto over civil and military offices. The

Book of Common Prayer was to be retained but not mandatory, and the power of bishops reduced. However, the *Heads of Proposals* were never presented to the king. Instead, parliament presented the much stricter *Newcastle Propositions*, which the king rejected, stating his preference for the softer *Heads of Proposals*. One comparative example must suffice to explain the gulf between the two. The *Heads of Proposals* suggested that parliament would control the army, including appointments to senior rank, for ten years. The *Newcastle Propositions*, by contrast, advocated this period of parliamentary control should be not less than twenty years. In seemingly opting for the former, and rejecting the latter, the king exploited a gap within the ranks of those opposed to him. Levellers such as John Lilburne, who had previously been indebted to Cromwell for securing his freedom, now saw his and Ireton's negotiation with the king as a betrayal.[44] Thus, the king temporarily divided his enemies whilst making plans for another civil war. In this second round of conflict in 1648, sometimes called the second civil war, the independents in the New Model Army found themselves fighting three sets of enemies: die-hard royalists, their numbers boosted by ex-parliamentarians; Presbyterians in parliament; and Levellers within the ranks of the army. Each of these mini-wars was won by force of arms. The royalist uprisings in Kent, Essex and elsewhere were crushed. Parliament was purged of Presbyterians by force of arms. However, the Levellers remained a nagging problem.

On 27 April 1649, a military execution took place in front of St Paul's Cathedral. The condemned man was a non-commissioned officer of the New Model Army in his early twenties. His name was Robert Lockyer, and his offence was mutiny. Lockyer was a Leveller and his regiment, Colonel Whalley's, had been quartered in Bishopsgate, pending fresh orders. There was talk of the regiment being sent to Ireland, but the troopers were angry about their continuing arrears of pay. Lockyer and his cohort barricaded themselves into an alehouse, the Black Bull, in Islington. They refused to come out unless their arrears were paid. The situation escalated and Thomas Fairfax and Oliver Cromwell, the two most senior army officers, were summoned. The mutineers were eventually coaxed out and six, including Lockyer, were condemned to death, to discourage other potential mutineers. However, Cromwell appealed to Fairfax for mercy and, with the exception of Lockyer, who was the ringleader, the others were spared. Lockyer was sentenced to a very public death by firing squad. Fairfax was a hard man to cross. During the royalist uprising at Colchester in the summer of 1648, Fairfax was commanding the regiments of the New Model Army that besieged the town. After eleven weeks, the royalists surrendered. Two of the royalist commanders were Sir Charles Lucas and Sir John Lisle. Earlier in the civil war, both men had been captured and released on giving their parole not to take up arms against parliament. Immediately after the surrender, Lucas and Lisle were court-martialled. Found guilty of breaking parole and maintaining a siege beyond reasonable hope of relief, they were executed.[45] The message was simple: defy parliament and the army at your peril.

The Levellers were not stereotypical rabble rousers. The movement originated in the thinking, educated merchant classes and professions. John Bastwick, for example, studied at Emmanuel College, and then obtained a medical degree at the University of Padua. His practice was in Colchester and it is likely that living in this radical Essex town influenced his growing puritanism.[46] The Leveller ideal may well have spread its support base to those below, but it was a child of the 'middling sort'. Immunity from prosecution for actions during the civil war, freedom of worship, and voting rights for a parliament accountable to the people were its goals. Like 'roundhead' the term 'Leveller' began as a nickname.[47] The Levellers started to tear up the fabric of society to build a new, better society. Robert Lockyer was a case in point. Confirmed into the Baptist church at the age of 16, he joined the parliamentarian army in 1642. Lockyer served in Colonel Whalley's regiment of cavalry at Naseby and Colchester.[48] However, Lockyer was also present at the Leveller meetings at Ware, and his own regiment was known for electing radical agitators in 1647.[49] It has been speculated that Lockyer's association with the Levellers sealed his fate.[50] Fairfax and probably Cromwell were not social revolutionaries. Cromwell's antipathy to the Levellers is well-recorded and Fairfax was playing the role expected of the nobility, supporting the government of the day and maintaining social order.[51] What happened next confirmed fears about the popularity of the Leveller movement.

Robert Lockyer's funeral was one of the most spectacular of the civil wars. It was one of a series of political funerals that defined the revolution. As Ian Gentles points out, since the turn of the fifteenth century, London with its long, wide streets provided a first-class venue for parades, royal entries and coronations, the lord mayor's show, state openings of parliament, and the biggest and most important, funeral processions.[52] As the civil wars progressed, the status of the political funeral went down the social scale. In other words, the 'honour' was accorded to those of lower social rank as well as nobility and royalty. In death, everybody was equal, as some thought they should be in life, and were therefore accorded equal honours. The pomp and circumstance accorded to Robert Devereux, Earl of Essex, the first commander of the London Regiments in the civil war and the first to voluntarily excuse himself under the Self-Denying Ordinance, is understandable and in keeping with established practice, likewise, that of John Pym MP, after his long service to parliament. However, the game-changers were the funerals of two Levellers. That of Admiral Rainsborough was impressive, as befits a senior officer. However, part of London stood still for the funeral of Robert Lockyer, a non-commissioned officer. A procession of at least 3,000 people, including parliamentarian soldiers, many with the black and green ribbons of the Levellers in their hats, filed through the city to Moorgate.[53] Whereas the funerals of Essex and Pym were commemorative, those of Rainsborough and Lockyer were protests.[54]

Although the Levellers were eventually crushed and lost their short war with the establishment, achieving some of their long-term goals meant they won the peace. The advent of mechanical printing, the temporary breakdown of centralised government censorship, thanks to the Stationers' Company, plus tenacious and indefatigable petitioning and pamphleteering to get their messages out into the wider worlds, were essential for this to happen.

Chapter 7

London's brave boys:
the trained bands and the defence of London

Before the civil war and again during the civil war, when the city acted parliament reacted. This applies to military matters as well as religious concerns. Initiatives originating in the city were belatedly approved by parliament. It was, of course, entirely natural that the capital should be a major driver in the parliamentarian war machine. What is significant is that the city, the commercial hub of London, should by its actions, demonstrate its awareness of political, military and religious concerns.

The survey of London's defences during the civil war begins with possibly the most important question of all. How do you raise an army when there is no standing army? That was the vital question that parliamentarians and royalists both had to answer in the summer of 1642. Before the civil wars, there was no standing army in the three kingdoms. There were local militias, often formed at county level, which had existed since Saxon times. These were trained reservists, not dissimilar to the present day Territorial Army. In time, they acquired the title of 'trained bands'. They were called to muster for inspection several times a year and called to fight in times of war. In times of threatened war or invasion, they could be put on alert for a short time. When these threats had been dealt with, they were stood down. If the emergency persisted or escalated into war, the state simply impressed men to serve as soldiers or sailors as required.

Why did the crown not employ a full-time professional army instead of organising local bands of volunteers? There were many reasons. The country was neither at war nor facing threat of invasion all the time. Therefore, there was no need to have a permanent force on alert for fifty-two weeks of the year. While the crown was prepared to meet the cost of training and equipping a reserve force, it would not countenance paying and feeding men to remain idle for an unspecified length of time, as Wilfred Emberton notes.[1]

There were further considerations. The volunteers who formed the trained bands had their day-time occupations and families. If the trained bands had been a full-time force, the impact would have been felt upon local communities. Each man enlisted would have meant one man less to work the land, or sell his goods or supply services. In times of good harvests and trade, this may not be a problem. However, neither the harvest nor the flow of trade was consistent. In a time when your prosperity and your family's survival depended on optimising the harvest, taking men off the land was a policy that pointed to disaster. Similarly, the removal of men from their trade may have alleviated seasonal unemployment, but equally could cause disruption to the local community and its economy. Therefore, the trained bands continued as a part-time volunteer force. The crown claimed to have discharged its duty of supplying a defence as inexpensively as possible.

By the turn of the seventeenth century, trained bands had been absorbed into the fabric of society. Standards were minimal. Men and weapons were formally inspected one or twice a year at the general musters. The muster master, appointed by the lord lieutenant of the county, was responsible for appointing officers, training and submitting a return of manpower and the state of the weaponry held.[2] This meant that the social makeup of the bands more or less followed the social structure of the day. Officers were predominantly men of money and position, while the rank and file tended to be working men. Hardworking, honest and doubtless including skilled and successful men, but ultimately their lower military rank mirrored their social rank in relation to their military superiors. However, this cosy arrangement didn't necessarily apply in London, where the officers and ranks of the London bands were drawn from a somewhat more mixed social pool, an anomaly that became increasingly visible during the civil war years.

How were the trained bands funded? Up to the mid-sixteenth century, command of a trained band was deemed to be a royal appointment and was therefore funded by the crown. However, during Elizabeth I's reign, this funding structure changed. Although serving in the name of Queen Elizabeth, the duty of appointing officers was delegated to the lord lieutenants of the counties. By the turn of the seventeenth century, the financial responsibility for funding the trained bands had similarly been outsourced. The art of leadership is delegation, and this pragmatic and thrifty approach to matters of defence suited James I perfectly. Whilst James was energetic in his attempts to reform the church in his kingdoms, and to persuade parliament that in parliamentary debates less is more, he was pacific in military matters and preferred lasting peace to equipping armies.

This arrangement of delegating management and funding relieved the crown of a financial burden at the expense of the county ratepayers. Looking further ahead to the 1630s and Charles' extension of ship and coat-and-conduct money, it becomes easier to understand two issues. Firstly, the resistance to paying these two taxes started in the counties and spread inland as the remit of the taxes increased. Secondly, the county ratepayers were now paying multiple sets of taxes for forces that were rarely used. The smouldering embers of resentment towards royal policies in the counties during the 1630s were evident before sparks ignited in the towns and cities, as Lucy Hutchinson notes.[3] County ratepayers were naturally keen to keep their costs of maintaining their trained bands as low as possible, a policy that sometimes resulted in their defaulting in payment until the government reminded them of their responsibilities.[4]

Here again we find that London was the exception that proved the rule. The city resisted royal efforts to compel them to appoint a muster master in 1635. Over the next three years, correspondence flew back and forth between the city and the king. The king attempted to make muster master of the City of London a royal appointment. However, the city fathers stood firm and refused to accept the king's nomination of Captain John Fisher. The king's response was to write to Lord Mayor Richard Venn[5] in 1638, ordering him to ratify Fisher's appointment.[6] It is no coincidence that Richard Venn, who ironically had been knighted by the king just months earlier, was also the master of the Worshipful Company of Haberdashers, the most militant livery company in the city. During the civil war years, the haberdashers demonstrated their militancy.

By 1640, however, political strains in the three kingdoms necessitated a change of policy. The city supported the king's efforts in the bishops' wars, but only to a point. The king requested a loan from the City of London of £200,000 to finance the bishops' wars. The city assented to the loan but not to the amount asked. The king got £50,000. It was hoped that the shortfall would force the king to recall parliament to make up the difference in funding. It was equally likely that nobody expected the king to have to call two parliaments in 1640.

How were the London trained bands structured? From the year 1616 to the outbreak of civil war in 1642, the command structure was as follows: four regiments, each commanded by a colonel, each regiment consisting of five companies led by a captain. The four regiments were named after the four magnetic compass points: north, east, south and west. Their combined strength was 6,000 men.[7] Each company was allocated to a specific ward in the city, and each regiment was given a designated rendezvous point. For example, in 1616, Colonel Sir Thomas Lowe, haberdasher, alderman, and MP for London from 1606 to 1611,[8] commanded the East Regiment, and Captain Bond's company patrolled Aldgate Ward. Martin Bond was a merchant adventurer, later a haberdasher. He served as a common councillor and alderman for Aldgate and various other positions in the city, including president of St Bartholomew's Hospital.[9] The East Regiment's rendezvous point was between Leadenhall Street and St Mary Axe.[10]

The trained bands had another function besides that of being on call to defend the capital from military attack. In the absence of a police force, law and order in the city was operated through a system of parish and ward constables, who ensured the good citizens of London kept the king's peace. There was another ward officer known as the beadle, who had civic duties and intervened in minor disturbances of the peace. Constables, however, could arrest people and bring them before magistrates. In times of serious disorder, the lord mayor could call out the trained bands to restore order. However, this privilege was taken away in early January 1642. The king's ill-conceived pursuit of the five members into the city and the now suspect loyalties of Lord Mayor Richard Gurney prompted parliament to pass the Militia Ordinance, which effectively took control of the London trained bands out of the lord mayor's hands.[11]

In 1643, however, under the pressure of months of civil war, the structure of the London trained bands had changed dramatically. The four peace-time regiments were expanded to six, and named after colours rather than points of the compass. A further three regiments were formed from the suburbs of Tower Hamlets, Westminster and Southwark, plus auxiliary regiments, all authorised by an ordinance of parliament issued in April 1643, placing them under the control of the Committee for Militia in London:

> *And these Volunteers being Listed, Armed, Exercised, and formed into Regiments, might be in the nature of Auxiliaries to the Trained bands of the said City, for the good ends and purposes before mentioned. All which is conceived may be the better effected if the same new Forces may according to their desires be within the ordering and disposal of the Committee for the Militia of the said City: For the better securing therefore of the Parliament, and City[12].*

The general muster of the London military held on 26 September 1643 records that each London regiment was commanded by a colonel, assisted by a colonel's captain and lieutenant-colonel. The six London regiments now consisted of four companies, led by a captain.[13] The unknown compiler of this muster evidently had strong connections to the city and its regiments because, unlike the regiments of the suburbs, he annotated the names and ranks of the officers and non-commissioned officers with brief descriptions of their occupations and where they worked in the city: Lieutenant-Colonel Ralph Harrison, uncle of later regicide Major-General Thomas Harrison, of the Yellow Regiment, for example, is recorded as being 'A Woollen Draper in Fleet Street', and Sergeant-Major Owen Roe, of the Green Regiment is described as 'A Mercer in Cheapside'.[14]

By autumn 1643, the parliamentarians had decided these regiments were not always needed for the defence of the capital. The aftermath of Edgehill in October 1642 dissipated royalist morale and resistance in the city. The successful repulse of the king's forces at Turnham Green in November that year proved the city could not be taken, especially after London's defences, the lines of communication, were erected. The lack of resistance from within London freed up the London regiments to take their campaign on the road. Leaving just one regiment in London, as a precaution, the parliamentarian commanders were grateful for the boost in manpower.

Cometh the hour, cometh the man. Major-General, short for Sergeant-Major-General, Philip Skippon was a professional soldier who had considerable experience fighting in the Thirty Years War. Skippon was a man of relatively little formal education. Clarendon writes that Skippon was 'a man of order and sobriety', having worked his way up the ranks from 'common soldier' to 'the reputation of a good officer'. However, Clarendon adds the slur that Skippon was illiterate.[15] This is questionable and it has been counter-asserted that Skippon was a highly religious man who kept a copy of Breeches' bible, in which he marked passages in ink.[16] Annotating books is considered to be a hallmark of the scholar. Although it's unlikely that Skippon received a classical education, after twenty years practical soldiering in the pressure cooker that was early seventeenth-century Europe, he certainly knew his business on the battlefield. His religious convictions, military knowledge and self-discipline were qualities that would be drilled into the soldiers of the New Model Army later in the civil wars.

Ironically, Skippon's experience of campaigning gained in the Thirty Years War nearly disqualified him from obtaining a field command early in the civil war. The parliamentarian councils of war were reluctant to risk losing one of their most experienced commanders and Skippon did not appear at Edgehill or Brentford. However, in November 1642, Skippon led his troops, some of whom were greener than the grass at Turnham Green, exhorting them forward with the demonstrable promise that as their commander he shared the same risks in discharging their duty to God. This was important to stabilise the militiamen of the trained bands, where there was more enthusiasm than experience – city merchants and tradesmen of all descriptions, with hands more used to working with pen and tools rather than wielding unfamiliar weapons. The nursery rhyme *Three Fools in a*

Tub, although published in the eighteenth century, contains the lines 'The butcher, the baker, the candlestick maker', which may well have accurately described the occupations of just three of the soldiers in the London bands.[17]

The Battle of Turnham Green was a turning point in the outcome of the civil war. The repulse of the royalist army finally gave the parliamentarian forces a victory to celebrate, after the inconclusive draw at Edgehill in October and the battering defeat inflicted by Prince Rupert's troops at Brentford only days before. Turnham Green was one of the most significant battles of the civil wars. Admittedly, the royalist army was not destroyed as at Naseby in 1645. However, the king's army was decisively repulsed. London's boys stood their ground and the city's defences were never tested in battle. Tactically and strategically, this was a solid victory for parliament and London. The eighteenth-century stationer and topographer John Noorthouck neatly summarised these events in *A New History of London Including Westminster and Southwark*, published in 1773:

> *After the engagement at Edgehill, the king advanced as near as Reading, and afterward to Colnbrook, where the parliament sent him fresh overtures for an accommodation. Charles agreed to enter into a treaty; and Essex by hasty marches reached London. The parliament sent orders to their troops for a cessation of arms, expecting the like on the king's part; but the next day under cover of a thick mist, he advanced to Brentford, hoping to surprise the train of artillery then at Hammersmith; and finally, the parliament and city: he was however, unexpectedly and vigorously repulsed by a party which lay at Brentford. This attack, while a treaty was depending, caused a general consternation; Essex immediately drew his forces together, to stop the king's progress; and an order being sent to the city for the trained bands to be drawn out, they marched immediately under major Skippon, and joined the earl of Essex, at Turnham Green; which induced the king to retire to Oxford.*[18]

The longer-term implications of this parliamentarian victory, just 6 miles from London, were yet to unfold, but several themes emerged. The royalists set-up their headquarters in the ancient university town of Oxford, over 50 miles from London as the crow flies. Logistically, this meant that London was at least a week's march from Oxford by horse and foot, assuming good weather and clear roads. Secondly, although nobody realised at the time, the royalists would never attempt to attack London again throughout the civil war. Arguably, the royalists had thrown away their best chance of taking London after Edgehill, when both sides retired from the field leaving the road to London open. However, the parliamentarians in the city were not taking any chances and on 23 February 1643, common council ordered London to be fortified against a royalist attack, as John Noorthouck describes:

> The conduct of the city was now decisive: by order of the common council, the city wall was cleared of all sheds and buildings without; its bulwarks were repaired and mounted with artillery, and new works added at the parts most exposed. The parliament that confirmed this act of common council, March 7, extended the plan of fortification so as to include London, Westminster, and Southwark. They were surrounded by a chain of forts, connected by lines of communication; all the ways leading to the city were stopped up, excepting those entering at Charing Cross, St. Giles's in the fields, St. John's-street, Shoreditch, and Whitechapel; the extremities of which streets were fortified with breastworks, musket proof. For the expense of these great works, eight fifteenths were levied on all the wards in the city; and they were prosecuted with such alacrity, that the ramparts and redoubts were completed in a short space of time.[19]

As city surveyor and historian Norman G. Brett-James notes, the fortifications erected in 1643 were an extension and consolidation of the defences put into place in the summer and early autumn of 1642.[20] It is also significant that the improvements in the London fortifications were ordered by common council, an initiative that parliament later ratified, rather than parliament ordering the city to carry out the work. As Brett-James observed:

> The City authorities realised from the first the need for adequate defence and had the old wall put in a state of security, and prepared to construct fortifications farther out in order to protect the suburbs as well as the City.[21]

The lines of communication were erected in 1643 and, although never tested in battle with the king's forces, stood firm throughout the civil wars. Their construction aroused much interest in London and beyond. Sometimes this was idle curiosity, as when the Venetian Ambassador noted:

> They do not cease to provide with energy for the defence of London. There is no street, however little frequented, that is not barricaded with heavy chains, and every post is guarded by numerous squadrons. At the approaches to London they are putting up great trenches and small forts of earthworks at which a great number of people are at work, including the women and little children.[22]

Other eyes were taking note of what was being built and where. During the initial phase of building, in 1642, the royalist Sir Kenelm Digby was arrested after taking rather too much interest in construction work at Mile End, and in his capacity as deputy surveyor of works, another royalist, John Webb, sent sketches of the defences to the king.[23] However, the existence of the lines could not be kept secret. Once erected, they stood for all to see, which may have been a factor in the king's decision not to attempt to attack London, but to play a longer game of siege and starvation to bring his errant capital to heel. This strategy failed, however, and London survived the civil war without its defences being assailed.

However, despite surviving the war, the lines could not survive the uneasy truce that existed in 1646/47. They were ordered to be 'slighted', which means any features that could be used to maintain a defensive position, such as a parapet, was dismantled in September 1647, when the recently politicised New Model Army marched into London to claim their arrears of pay. The city that had supported the parliamentarian armies between 1642 and 1646 was now asking why this force persisted when the king's field armies had surrendered, and was uneasy about the political fighting machine it had created:

> *Be it Ordained, by the Lords and Commons in Parliament assembled, That the Lines of Communication about the Cities of London and Westminster and the Borough of Southwark, and the Parts adjacent, and all the Forts upon and about the same, be forthwith slighted and demolished; and that the Committee of the Militia of London, settled by Ordinance of Parliament this present Second Day of September, do see this Ordinance put in Execution with all possible Expedition; and that they do receive Advice from Sir Thomas Fairfax in the Way of their Proceedings in this Service.*[24]

This, however, wasn't a total demolition of walls and defences, such as was ordered after the siege of Colchester in 1648. A basic defensive ring was maintained and even slightly enhanced during the royalist uprising in 1648. This was augmented with an artillery battery at Whitehall in 1650. These defences were maintained until the royalists were defeated after Worcester in 1651. By 1653, the Council of State ordered the ordinance in London to be placed in the Tower of London.[25] Regrettably for historians, the work of demolishing the defences of London was carried out too well. The ravages of time since the civil wars means that almost nothing tangible, beyond some scattered remains in Hyde Park and a handful of sketches and maps, survives today.[26]

But in spring 1643, the parliamentarians were right in taking precautions against a royalist attack on the capital. The cheerful optimism that believed the war would be over by Christmas was shattered by the events following Edgehill. In the long years of war that followed, securing London at an early stage was a massive strategic victory for the parliamentarians. The London trained bands could now be ordered to march out of the city to areas of the country they may never have visited previously in their lives. Given the premise there is a fine dividing line between local pride and insularity, it can be argued that it was at this point that the civil wars stopped being a military standoff between king and parliament punctuated by local conflicts, but finally emerged for what it was: a national civil war. In this enlarged conflict, the London regiments marched out of the city and into justified fame. In August 1643, 'Skippon's brave boys' cheerfully tramped halfway across England to assist the parliamentarian forces under Essex to raise the royalist siege of Gloucester. Parliament ordered that:

> *Six Regiments of Foot, consisting of Eight Thousand Men, or any less Number, as likewise Fifteen Hundred Horse, or any less Number, either of their trained bands, Auxiliaries, or other Forces under the Command of the said Committee, within the Cities of London and Westminster. And all other Forces within the Forts or Lines of Communication, and the Parishes mentioned in the Weekly Bill of Mortality, to march, according to the Discipline and Order of War, under the Conduct and Command of such Colonels, Lieutenant Colonels, Captains, and other Officers, as the same Committee shall nominate and appoint, with all necessary Provisions of Arms, Ordnance Ammunition, and other Carriages, from the City of London, and Places afore-mentioned, unto the Lord General the Earl of Essex, wheresoever he shall be; to proceed for the Relief of the City of Gloucester.*[27]

This was the instruction from parliament. In London, the city responded with enthusiasm and, as John Noorthouck writes, issued the following instructions towards the cause:

> *The relief of Gloucester was now the object of immediate consideration: The common council ordered the city companies to advance 50,000l. More; all shops within the lines of communication were commanded to be shut until the siege of Gloucester was raised; and six regiments, one of horse, two of trained bands, and three of auxiliaries, raised with amazing speed, joined the main army under Essex, to effect this important object.*[28]

The raising of the siege of Gloucester in September 1643 was more than a timely boost for the parliamentarian armies, and a temporary check to the momentum enjoyed by the royalists after their successful summer campaign. At this point in the war, the parliamentarians badly needed a victory after successive defeats at Adwalton Moor, Lansdowne, Roundaway Down and Bristol throughout June and July 1643. In August 1643, the London regiments' brave stand at Turnham Green the previous November was a distant memory. The king's armies were cutting through their parliamentarian opponents in the south-west like hot knives through butter. If Gloucester fell, the king might have established a bridgehead in the River Severn and could unite and co-ordinate his royalist followers in Wales and Cornwall.[29] The success or failure of the parliamentarian defence of Gloucester was therefore a potential game-changer, a tipping point in the civil war.

The equation, however, wasn't a simple win or lose scenario. If Gloucester fell, it potentially meant parliament losing the war. On the other hand, victory at Gloucester wouldn't generate the impetus for parliament to sweep to victory but may buy precious time for the battered parliamentarian armies to rest, recover and rethink their strategies. This message was not lost on London and it was just as much in London's interest as Gloucester's that the London regiments were ordered west, to assist in the relief of their parliamentarian comrades. Following their fine victory at Gloucester, Essex began the long march to London. The king reacted and scrambled his army to pursue Essex, overtaking them at Newbury on 20 September. Neither side could press an advantage and, tactically, the battle was drawn. From the parliamentarian point of view, however, Newbury was a strategic victory because it enabled Essex to bring his tired force home to London.[30]

In September 1643, Gloucester and Newbury were timely achievements for the parliamentarian armies. Morale in the parliamentarians' camp had been plummeting with each defeat that summer and, on 5 August 1643, the Lords seriously considered offering the king their propositions for surrender:

My Lords believe that it is too visible to the Understanding of all Persons, that this Kingdom, with all those Blessings of Plenty and Abundance, the Fruits of our long and happy Peace, must be forthwith turned into the Desolation and Famine that accompany a Civil War; and that those Hands and Hearts, which should secure this Land, do now endanger it, by our unnatural Division; which Considerations have moved my Lords to return again Propositions to His Majesty, in the which they do desire your Concurrence; the Reasonableness and Justice of them being such as, if

they be rejected, our Cause may thereby be strengthened, and the Kingdom
encouraged to preserve themselves in their just Rights.[31]

When the Lords' proposal was put to the Commons on 7 August 1643, the
House was divided. Although the 'yeas', those supporting the Lords, carried
the vote by eighty-one votes to seventy-nine, a wafer-thin majority of two, the
votes were disputed and a second division was called. After this second vote,
the proposal for peace terms was rejected by eighty-eight votes to eighty-one,
indicating that, allowing for members changing their minds, nine members
who abstained from voting in the first division certainly voted against it in the
second. Thus, parliament voted to continue the war by a mere seven votes.
The Commons also moved to distance themselves from the Lords' position
on the matter of peace negotiations with the king and appointed a committee
to meet with and explain their reasons to the Upper House.[32]

Further incidents followed. On 8 August, London housewives, angry about
wartime taxation and higher food prices, marched to protest before parliament
and present a petition calling for peace with the king.[33] The women were
armed with brickbats and when the petition was rejected, they rioted in New
Palace Yard. The besieged members of parliament decided that discretion
was the greater part of valour and locked themselves indoors. Dragoons were
mobilised and, when the riot was quelled, two women lay dead and many
more were nursing their injuries. A week later, seven peers abandoned the
parliamentarian cause and joined the king. The welcome, and long overdue,
news of the parliamentarian victory at Gloucester after a summer of defeat
and turmoil therefore came none too soon.[34] On 7 August, the same day the
Commons voted on the Lords' proposals, the House received a delegation of
common councillors, headed by Alderman Atkins, who presented a petition
regarding the safety of the city. The Commons thanked the city for its support
during the ongoing crisis and further responded by ordering:

That the Committee formerly appointed to meet with the Committee of
the Militia of London, shall have Power to receive from the City such
Propositions as shall be offered unto them for the Safety of the City, and
Peace of the Kingdom; and to prepare the Draught of an Ordinance upon
those Propositions; and to present it to the House.[35]

The Commons also recommended that the lord mayor take action to prevent
further disturbances or 'tumults'.[36] The housewives' riot at Westminster
certainly fitted that description and it is extremely likely that, had the melee

in New Palace Yard taken place before the crucial second vote to continue the war, the Commons may have voted with the Lords to seek a negotiated settlement with the king. It is also important to remember that, at frequent intervals during the civil wars, parliament offered the king peace terms. In January 1643, unsuccessful peace negotiations had been attempted with the Treaty of Oxford. The king had assented to negotiate, granting the commissioners of the peace delegation safe conduct.[37]

The Treaty of Oxford was a repackaged version of the *Nineteen Propositions* that was intended to curtail royal powers by transferring them to parliament. It was a last gasp attempt to avert civil war. Its key points were that parliament was to have control over the armed forces, supervise foreign policy and the education of the king's children. Laws against Roman Catholics were to be tightened up. The five members were to be pardoned and the House of Commons given the right of veto to new peers sitting in the House of Lords[38]. These propositions had been presented to the king in June 1642 and summarily rejected. Two months later, the king and parliament were at war. However carefully they were rewritten and presented, the terms in the Treaty of Oxford were as unpalatable to the king in January 1643 as the propositions had been in summer 1642 and, unsurprisingly, were refused. Shortly before Turnham Green, the king marched on, thus avoiding a delegation from parliament that sought to find common ground whereby each side might step back with honour.[39]

The London trained bands also operated in the Home Counties around London and in December 1643, parliament ordered the regiments be ready to march into Middlesex and Surrey and elsewhere, for the 'defence of the cities of London and Westminster, and parts adjacent'.

> *That the Committee of the Militia of the City of London shall have power, and is hereby authorized to Command the White and Yellow Regiments of the trained bands of the said City, and such other Regiments of trained bands and Auxiliaries of Foot, and as many Troops of Horse, or other Forces, under their commands within the Cities of London and Westminster Lines of Communication, and Parishes mentioned in the weekly Bills of Mortality, as to them shall seem convenient; to March under the conduct of Richard Browne Esquire, Major-General of this Brigade, who is hereby authorized by the said Lords and Commons, to lead and conduct them for the defence of the Cities of London and Westminster, and parts adjacent, into the Counties of Middlesex and Surrey and elsewhere, as he shall be directed by the Committee of the Militia, or Sir William Waller, with the consent of the said Committee.[40]*

This cleverly worded ordinance was a reassurance to the men of the London regiments that their duties were in defence of London and would not take them far from their homes, businesses and loved ones. In what would nowadays be described as the 'small print', it also enabled the London regiments to be deployed further afield as the qualifying phrases 'and elsewhere' and 'directed by the Committee of the Militia' indicates. Throughout the great campaigns that took place in 1644, such as Chariton, where John Hampden was killed on 29 March, and Marston Moor on 2 July, the three senior generals Essex, Manchester and Waller regularly called upon the London regiments for their assistance.[41]

In military terms, the year 1644 was the mirror image of 1643. Except that parliament had the better of the year in terms of victories but threw away their chance of a final victory in late October. By now, the Scots army had entered England and were fighting with the English parliamentarians. Others had arrived. The king's Irish army had been freed up from fighting the rebels in Ireland, thanks to the king's under-the-table deal with the Confederation of Kilkenny. The civil wars were now the wars of three kingdoms. For the first half of the year, parliament won a series of victories that included Nantwich, Cheriton and Selby. However, things unravelled somewhat on 29 June when Sir William Waller's force was unexpectedly beaten at Copredy Bridge. The Tower Hamlets Regiment and its near neighbours the Kentish Regiments acquitted themselves well, as the official report to parliament states: 'the Bridge being made good and secured for their Retreat by the Regiments of the Tower-Hamlets.'[42] This rear-guard action prevented the defeat of Waller's army becoming a rout as Emberton notes.[43] Meanwhile, Waller tidied up the surviving portions of his army and the Tower Hamlets Regiment, having proved their value to the campaign, albeit in less than glorious circumstances, prepared to march home:

Waller after his Forces were got back over the Bridge, maintained it, and kept his Men drawn up, and both Armies faced one another the rest of that day, and the Cannons plaid on each side; in the Night they alarmed each other, but little Execution done, and in the Morning the King's Army was drawn off, and Waller marched over Cropedy-Bridge, and so on Tuesday the 2d of July to Towcester, where Major-General Brown met them, but marched with them only till Thursday towards Northampton, and then marched away to the Siege of Greenland-House, and on the 11th of July the Regiments of London Auxiliaries that went forth with Waller, May the 12th, came home again to the City.[44]

The month of July promised better news. The combined Anglo-Scots army comfortably defeated Rupert at Marston Moor on 2 July, and later that month, the royalist stronghold of York surrendered.[45] Unfortunately for the parliamentarians, that was as good as it was going to get that summer. Just two months after Marston Moor, Essex's army disintegrated at Lostwithiel, the lord general ignominiously fleeing by boat.[46]

Lieutenant-Colonel Oliver Cromwell, the rising star of the parliamentarian cavalry, argued with Lord General Manchester about whether to fight on or talk with the king for peace. Manchester argued, 'If we beat the king nine and ninety times, he is still the king, but if he beats us once we shall be hanged and our posterity undone.'

Cromwell replied: 'If so my Lord, why did we take up arms?' and their argument continued.[47]

Meanwhile, the Second Battle of Newbury took place on 27 October 1644. This battle was also a draw, but this time the advantage was with the royalists, because the king recovered some ordinance.[48] The king and Waller had chased each other's armies around for two months without any tangible result.

The royalist defeat at Marston Moor in June was actually an enforced retreat. By autumn that year, Rupert had gathered and rallied his scattered forces and the king had recovered quite some ground, militarily and politically. In contrast, William Waller's military career was effectively over after the second draw at Newbury. Although still a major-general, he acted in a minor capacity for the remainder of his commission. However, Waller had one last contribution to the war effort.

On 2 July, Waller wrote to the Committee of Both Kingdoms and suggested remodelling the separate parliamentarian armies into one. This new army would be known as the New Model Army.[49] The Second Battle of Newbury was therefore one of the last occasions in the civil wars when the London regiments fought under their own banners. But in January 1645, when parliament finally passed the Self-Denying Ordinance and then the New Model Army was created, officers and men from London were there, under the command of Philip Skippon. Unlike Essex and Waller, Skippon kept his command. Some of Skippon's brave boys would march again in the ranks of the New Model Army. The appointment of Philip Skippon to command the London regiments was a masterstroke by the parliamentarians. His experience as a fighting soldier, religious views and personal courage were almost certainly major factors in the civil war record of the London regiments.

Chapter 8

To the winner the spoils:
some later lives of stakeholders

L ieutenant-General Oliver Cromwell succeeded Lord Fairfax as commander-in-chief of the New Model Army. Despite prayers for peace at Christchurch Greyfriars in the summer of 1649, further rebellion raged in Scotland and Ireland, where Cromwell commanded in campaigns noted as much for bloodshed as military skill. However, Cromwell the politician was less successful than Cromwell the soldier. Despite his political and military inexperience, Cromwell had moved smartly through the ranks of parliament and the army. His initiation into parliament had been brief. However, the questionably dressed farmer who sat in the parliament of 1628–29 would have learnt much about the relationship between Stuart kings and parliaments. Eleven long years passed before Cromwell's career as a parliamentarian would continue and, like others, he found his career cut short by the dissolution of the short parliament. Cromwell was therefore still relatively inexperienced when he sat as MP for the third time in the long parliament. His third spell in the Commons would prove to be a career-defining era for Cromwell, parliament and the three kingdoms.

> *The death of the king, who was executed January 30th, was followed by the dissolution of monarchical government. The house of commons passed a vote for the abolishment of the house of lords, as useless and dangerous, and another for the abolishment of monarchy: the forms of all public business were altered from being in the king's name, to that of the keepers of the liberties of England: and it was declared high treason, to proclaim or otherwise acknowledge Charles Stuart, commonly called prince of Wales. Even the king's statues at St. Paul's and in the Royal Exchange were pulled down, and in the niche of the latter was placed the following inscription Exit tyrannus, regum ultimus "the tyrant, the last of the kings, is gone.*[1]

Despite the execution of the king, the proclamation of a commonwealth and the abolition of the House of Lords in 1649, the three kingdoms were far from settled. The royalists had finally been defeated in England, but they had temporarily been replaced by the threat posed to the new republic by the Levellers. These were gradually being suppressed as the Commonwealth sought to establish its authority. The independent party, to which Cromwell belonged, controlled the purged parliament, although both parliament and the army were leavened with a sprinkling of die-hard Levellers and Fifth Monarchy Men. Defeated royalists who had either left the country or had been compounded and barred from public office, sometimes for life, retired to their estates. The towns and cities were controlled by parliament, including the great prize of London that had enabled the parliamentarians to win the war.

However, that still left Scotland and Ireland where the civil war continued. Ten years previously, in 1639, the king's ill-advised military excursion to Scotland in the bishops' wars led, indirectly, to the outbreak of the civil wars. Two tense years later, inspired by political manoeuvring in parliament that led to the execution of Earl Strafford, the king's right-hand man in Ireland, the Irish rebellion broke out. Civil war erupted in England a few months later in 1642. The years 1649 to 1651 saw further fighting in Ireland and Scotland. These were drawn-out and bloody campaigns that ended with controversial incidents taking place at Drogheda and Wexford in Ireland. This was the third civil war, that finished with the defeat, but not the capture of, Prince Charles when his royalist army was destroyed at Worcester in 1651. The prince famously escaped by hiding in an oak-tree while parliamentarian soldiers vainly searched the woods. He had a charmed life in battles. He had narrowly escaped being captured at Edgehill, his first battle of the civil war, and his luck held after Worcester. The prince, who had been declared king in Scotland, retired to the Netherlands, where he remained until summoned by Generals Monck and Fairfax when the Cromwellian regime finally collapsed in 1659. But what happened in the meantime?

From 1651 to 1653, the rump parliament, as it was later known, rumbled on with Oliver Cromwell sitting as head of the Council of State as well as commander-in-chief of the New Model Army. However, Cromwell's patience, like some of those under him, was not finite. On 20 April 1653, exasperated at the slow pace of reform in the purged parliament, Cromwell dissolved the rump.[2] In its place, he appointed a short-lived nominated assembly, nicknamed 'barebones parliament'. In December 1653, Cromwell was installed as lord protector of England, Scotland and Ireland. For the first time, this island group in the Atlantic had a written constitution as, theoretically, the lord protector's powers were limited by the document, the *Instrument of Government*, the first three articles of which state:

> *I. That the Supreme Legislative Authority of the Commonwealth of England, Scotland, and Ireland, and the Dominions thereunto belonging, shall be and reside in one Person, and the People assembled in Parliament; the Style of which Person shall be The Lord Protector of the Commonwealth of England, Scotland, and Ireland. II. The Exercise of the chief Magistracy, and the Administration of the Government over the said Countries and Dominions, and the People thereof, shall be in the Lord Protector, assisted with a Council, the Number whereof shall not exceed 21, nor be less than 13. III. That all Writs, Process, Commissions, Patents, Grants, and other Things, which now run in the Name and Style of The Keepers of the Liberty of England by Authority of Parliament, shall run in the Name and Style of the Lord Protector, from whom, for the future, shall be derived all Magistracy and Honours in these three Nations; and have the Power of Pardons (except in case of Murders and Treason) and Benefit of all Forfeitures for the public Use; and shall govern the said Countries and Dominions in all Things by the Advice of the Council, and according to these Presents and the Laws.*[3]

However, Cromwell's model of a republic at ease with itself was harder to realise. Two protectorate parliaments and a brief experiment in carrying out indirect government through appointed major-generals failed to deliver the constitutional panacea to the nation's ills of the previous decade.[4] However, the protectorate was acting and starting to look like a durable government. The elections to the protectorate parliaments returned Cromwellian supporters, such as in Colchester. The Corporation of Colchester had petitioned Cromwell for a new town charter. One of the key requests was to restore the gift of electing the town's MP to the corporation, instead of an open election by the freeholders and the corporation. In return, the Corporation of Colchester promised to elect the godly Cromwellian candidate Henry Barrington. Colchester had supported parliament during the first phase of the civil war, but was disgraced when the royalists took over the town in the second civil war in 1648.[5] This was their opportunity to erase that black mark and, incidentally, for the corporation to recover political control over the town.[6] Cromwell also issued charters to three city livery companies. The Worshipful Company of Hackney Carriage Drivers can trace its origin to legislation passed in Cromwell's first protectorate parliament in 1654:

> *Forasmuch as many Inconveniences do daily arise by reason of the late increase and great irregularity of Hackney Coaches and Hackney Coachmen in London, Westminster and the places thereabouts: For remedy thereof, Be it Ordained by his Highness the Lord Protector, with the consent of His Council, that from the four and twentieth day of June, One thousand six hundred fifty and four ensuing, the number of persons keeping Hackney-coaches and Hackney horses for Coaches, within the City of London, Westminster and six miles about the late lines of communication, do not exceed at one time two hundred; nor the Hackney-coaches to be used by them, three hundred; nor their Hackney Horses for Coaches do not exceed the number of six hundred. And for the better Ordering and Governing the said Hackney-coach-men, be it Ordained that the Government and Ordering of them shall from time to time be in the Court of Aldermen, of the City of London, in such manner as is hereby Ordained.[7]*

This evolution from interim administration to permanent government gathered pace and there was serious talk of offering Cromwell the crown in 1657. He refused, preferring to remain as lord protector.[8] By 1658, Cromwell was in poor health. The stress of his position and the hurly-burly of the civil war years had taken their toll. Cromwell died on 3 September 1658 and the protectorate passed to his son Richard.[9] Whereas Oliver had been an outstanding soldier and fair politician, Richard had not been trained for leadership. Unlike Oliver, who held together the different factions in his court by the force of his magnetic personality, Richard was ill-equipped to do so.[10] Richard Cromwell's protectorate lasted less than a year and it was the intervention of Monck that cleaned up the constitutional mess by calling the convention parliament in 1660 as preparation for restoring the monarchy.[11] Richard Cromwell was literally thrust to greatness by his father's will. Unfortunately, he lacked the political guile and common touch to reconcile the opposing forces: those who wished for further reform and those who wished for reconciliation. Ultimately undone by his inability to control the radical sects in the army, Richard Cromwell's government was effectively overthrown by the general council of officers.[12] During the restoration, Richard Cromwell stayed out of trouble, lying low in the Netherlands, just as Prince Charles had done during his exile in the 1650s. However, he may have had the last laugh. He lived until 1712 and in his 80s occasionally attended parliament, under a pseudonym. In doing so, Richard Cromwell, although a commoner, outlived his successors Charles II, who died in 1685, James II, who died in 1701, and William and Mary, who died in 1702 and 1694 respectively.

By the 1650s, all but two of the five members that Charles failed to arrest in January 1642 were dead. John Pym, leader of the long parliament's opposition to Charles, died of natural causes, probably cancer, in December 1643.[13] Pym's age prevented him taking a military role in the civil wars. His greatest contribution was brokering the Solemn League and Covenant with the Scots. He was rewarded in death with a funeral at Westminster Abbey. William Strode was one of his pallbearers.[14] John Hampden, the ship money martyr, was killed in battle, the only one of the five members to die in arms, at Chalgrove Field in June 1643. Hampden's death is something of a mystery. There are conflicting reports as to the nature of the wound that killed him. Was it a royalist musket ball or his own pistol exploding? Similarly, rumours as to his last words and the story of the king offering to send his surgeon to tend the stricken parliamentarian.[15] William Strode was appointed to the committee of Westminster Divines in January 1645, but died of fever in September that year. Parliament ordered he be accorded the honour of being buried in Westminster Abbey. However, in September 1661, it was ordered that his mortal remains be disinterred and reburied elsewhere.[16] That left Denzil Holles and Arthur Haselrig. Holles was one of the members excluded from being an MP in 1648. He kept a low profile abroad during the interregnum and re-emerged at the restoration. He became a privy councillor and lived until 1680.[17] Arthur Haselrig was a republican but not a Cromwellian. He fought with Cromwell in the Scottish campaign in 1650, and supported the king's death sentence, but refused to serve as a judge. The dissolution of the rump alienated Haselrig, who declined to take a post in the protectorate. He was elected MP for each of the three protectorate parliaments, but was only allowed to serve in Richard Cromwell's parliament. He died of natural causes whilst imprisoned in the Tower in 1661.[18] Edward Montague, later Earl Manchester, retired from political life during the interregnum. The House of Lords had been purged in December 1648 and abolished in January 1649. Not wishing to work for the Commonwealth, Manchester spent the 1650s quietly at home. He assisted with the restoration, resumed his career in the Lords and was awarded the prestigious honour of Knight of the Order of the Garter in 1661 and Fellow of the Royal Society in 1667. He died in 1671.

Of all the characters described so far, George Monck is perhaps the greatest example of the political trimmer. This is not necessarily negative. Monck was a man of his time and recognised that sticking too close to your political convictions for too long wasn't always a good thing. Monck had started the war supporting Charles.[19] After being captured and spending some months in prison, Monck converted to the parliamentarian cause in 1644/45.[20] Later, he became a Cromwellian and lent his considerable personal and political support to first enforcing then stabilising that cause.[21] Finally, when the Cromwellian regime collapsed in 1659, Monck turned again, from Cromwellian to pragmatist. His role in the restoration was rewarded with a title, First Duke of Albemarle.[22] Monck proved his credentials to the newly restored monarchy by giving evidence against former regicides, many of whom were ex-comrades in arms. During the second Anglo–Dutch war, Monck served as lord admiral, and also demonstrated his organisational acumen during the Great Plague and the Fire of London.[23] It was reported that when Monck died in 1671, it was in the manner of a Roman general, with his officers at his bedside.[24]

At the same time that Monck took control of what remained of the government, Fairfax emerged from his semi-retirement and together the two men planned what would become the restoration. Fairfax's role in the restoration was important, but short-lived. A controversial episode from the siege of Colchester in 1648 came back to haunt Fairfax and destroy his hopes of working with the young king. During the civil war, a royalist army led by Sir Charles Lucas and Sir John Lisle had fled into Colchester. The New Model Army besieged the town and the garrison only surrendered after eleven weeks. The defenders were literally starved into submission. Tensions ran high and the parliamentarian commanders were determined to make the fate of Colchester an example to others. The royalist commanders, Lucas and Lisle, were court-martialled and executed for breaching parole and breaking their promises not to take up arms against parliament.[25] The town was fined £12,000 in lieu of sack.[26] Despite his considerable contribution in assisting with the restoration, Fairfax slipped out of the public sphere in the 1660s. His political career was over. This broke Fairfax, whose sole ambition during the civil wars had been to force the king back to the negotiation table and thus enable the restoration, no pun intended, of the king-in-parliament, taking advice from the Lords and redressing grievances raised by the Commons – what we would nowadays call a constitutional monarchy. In failing health he lived quietly at home, dying in 1671, aged 59.[27]

Philip Skippon was called to be one of the king's judges in 1649, but the career soldier, like Fairfax, declined to serve. Skippon held civil and military rank during the interregnum. On 14 February 1649, Skippon was name-checked among the army officers nominated to the first Council of State.[28] In late June 1650, crisis was brewing in Scotland. Fairfax was troubled at invading the allies of parliament during the civil war and resigned his command on 26 June. Cromwell took over and Skippon was appointed to command London. Skippon's service in keeping London trouble-free in that difficult summer of 1648 showed he was a safe pair of hands to guard the capital.[29] In 1655, royalists were expelled from London and Westminster as the country was to be run by a network of major-generals. Skippon was appointed major-general for London.[30] Skippon also became an MP, as the member for Lyme in the 1654 and 1656 parliaments, though he rarely spoke. He sat in the Cromwellian House of Lords and helped proclaim Richard as Cromwell's successor in 1658. It's almost certain that Skippon demonstrably had little taste for politics. He was a professional soldier, not a speechmaker. In 1659, what remained of the reinstated long parliament summoned Skippon to parliament to be appointed his last military command:

> *Major General Skippon, a Member of Parliament, came, from his Place, up to the Clerk's Table: And, standing there, Mr. Speaker acquainted him with the great Trust reposed in him by the Parliament and Commonwealth; and that the Parliament and Commonwealth expected Faithfulness from him, according to his Trust, to the Parliament and Commonwealth: And thereupon Mr. Speaker delivered him his commission to be Major-General and Commander in Chief of all the Forces within the City of London, the late Lines of Communication, and Weekly Bills of Mortality.*[31]

When so many others had been dismissed or overlooked, this was a singular honour. A lifetime soldiering leavened with politics took its toll, however, and Skippon gradually eased himself into retirement. He died in 1660.[32]

What became of that troublesome gang of three, who for a while, were the cutting edge of the movement known as the Levellers? John Bastwick continued writing through the 1640s. In 1648, he fell out with John Lilburne and distanced himself from his former ally. He also sharply criticised the independents. Bastwick died in October 1654. His widow Susanna petitioned parliament for relief, and claimed monies that had been ordered to be paid to John Bastwick by the Lords. The Commons Journal for 16 November 1654 notes:

> *The humble Petition of Susanna Bastwick, the distressed Widow of John Bastwick, Doctor in Physic, and her Children, was this Day read. Resolved, that it be referred to a Committee to consider how the Sum of Five Thousand Pounds, in the Petition mentioned, may be satisfied to the Petitioners, with most Equality, Justice, and Expedition: And to report their Opinion to the*

House with Speed. Resolved, that it be referred to the Committee to whom the Powers and Proceedings of the Judges of Salters Hall are referred: And that Alderman Gibbs, Mr. Lechmere, Colonel Baines, Colonel Bridges, and Sir Wm. Strickland, be added to that Committee.[33]

William Prynne celebrated his release from prison in 1640 by prosecuting William Laud, who had prosecuted Prynne and his friends in the 1630s. However, Prynne's real love was writing pamphlets. He published and criticised the military, the independents, the regicide and compared Oliver Cromwell to Richard III, one usurper to another. Prynne was discharged from parliament during Pride's Purge and spent three years in prison in the early 1650s.[34] He supported the restoration and Charles II made him keeper of records in the Tower. However, Prynne could not suppress his urge to criticise and his next target was the bishops in the 1660s. His output was prolific. He wrote over 200 pamphlets and tracts during his lifetime. We can imagine him and his friends as modern-day newspaper journalists, their weekly columns in the Sunday newspapers dreaded by the authorities, but loved by their supporters, and making guest appearances on BBC television's *Question Time.* Prynne died in 1669 and was buried at Lincolns Inn.[35] The barrister had come home.

John Lilburne may have been a Leveller, but he supported neither the trial nor regicide. Liburne reasoned that the existence of the monarchy blocked the ambitions of the commanders of the military.[36] Trying and executing the king, therefore, did not improve matters for the common man. In a way it worsened them. The army commanders had already identified the Levellers as a threat. Lilburne published another tract, *England's New Chains Discovered.* He and three supporters were arrested and quizzed by the Council of State. Cromwell was overheard angrily shouting that unless the Levellers were broken, they would break the army, the kingdom, and undo the hard work of the civil war years.[37] Lilburne was later acquitted of treason, but the Leveller movement was finished. For the next few years, Lilburne tried his hand at various employments. However, he was in and out of trouble and prison. In 1655, he became a Quaker. Lilburne died in 1657, in Eltham at the age of 42.[38]

The Earl of Clarendon was another who was ultimately disappointed at the restoration. Born plain Mr Edward Hyde in 1608, he had been a moderately angry MP in the early days of the long parliament, but in 1642 had taken the king's colours. Initially getting on well with Charles I, Hyde was knighted in 1643. Hyde fell out with Charles in 1647 though, and retired to the Channel Islands. He greeted Prince Charles as the new King Charles II, when he was proclaimed as such by Sir George Carteret in 1649, and began work on his magnum opus, *The History of the Great Rebellion and Civil War*. At the restoration, Hyde was elevated to the aristocracy by Charles II. Clarendon was an important figure who had acquired political enemies. Political wrangling at court and accusations of fraud led to impeachment and he was exiled to France.[39] Clarendon died in Rouen in 1674 with his manuscript finished but unpublished. It would remain so, on his instructions, for nearly thirty years after his death. Clarendon's son, the Earl of Rochester, published *The History of the Rebellion* in volume format from 1702, with the stated intention of educating the present-day reader, rather than rebuking the characters who had played out the dramatic events of the civil wars.[40] Meanwhile, Clarendon's daughter Anne married Prince James, later James II. Their daughter, Clarendon's granddaughter, Anne, became Queen Anne, the last Stuart monarch, in 1702.[41]

Prince Rupert, the nephew of Charles I, survived the early years of the restoration. Despite his brilliance in the cat-and-mouse game with Essex in the Thames Valley in 1644, regrouping his scattered army after Marston Moor, and taking Leicester, he was finally defeated at Naseby in 1645. Despite this setback, Rupert was given command of Bristol, but Charles relieved him of command when Rupert surrendered the city as indefensible. From 1649 to 1652, Rupert acted as a royalist privateer, attacking English shipping and frequently running the gauntlet of Admiral Blake's fleet. Thereafter, Rupert retired from politics and spent time in Germany, experimenting in the new sciences. Charles II welcomed Rupert back at the restoration and he became a founder member of the Royal Society. Rupert was militarily active in the 1660s. The second Anglo-Dutch war kept him busy fighting at sea alongside his sometime parliamentarian foe Monck. Now, however, their former differences were long forgotten as fellow officers in the service of Charles II. However, like so many of his contemporaries on both sides of the conflict, the civil war years took their toll on his health and longevity. Rupert died at Westminster in 1680 aged 61 and was buried in Westminster Abbey.[42]

John Milton came close to not surviving the restoration. His political writings, such as *The Tenure of Kings and Magistrates*, published in 1649, was a dissertation on monarchs being called to account by their subjects and tacitly defended the execution of the king and regicide in general. His classical education and linguistic ability of being fluent in at least six languages, combined with his powers as a wordsmith, earned Milton the position of secretary of state for Foreign Tongues.[43] Despite failing eyesight, which resulted in him going blind in 1652, Milton continued working and writing, assisted by his amanuenses, notably Andrew Marvell. In 1658, Milton began the poem for which he is perhaps best known, *Paradise Lost*. Due to the upheaval caused by the end of the protectorate and the restoration, this took Milton five years to complete. During this time, he was fortunate not to be seriously embroiled in the reprisals levied against regicides and other supporters of the republic. Just on the cusp of the restoration, Milton unwisely published a tract, *The Ready and Easy Way to Establish a Free Commonwealth*. His republican writings, service to the Commonwealth and implied support for regicide brought Milton to the attention of the authorities. However, a spell in prison and payment of a large fine was deemed sufficient punishment for his past misdeeds.[44] It's almost certain that Milton's blindness and the intervention of friends such as Marvell, MP for Hull in the so–called cavalier parliament, saved him from a more severe sanction. Having finally finished *Paradise Lost* in 1663, it took Milton another four years to get it published. He received the sum of £10 and continued to write until shortly before his death in 1674.[45] Milton is buried in St Giles Cripplegate, less than a mile from his birthplace in Bread Street, off Cheapside.

William Juxon was the Bishop of London between 1633 and 1649. His superior, William Laud, was executed for treason in 1645. Juxon previously served as lord high treasurer of England, from 1636 to 1641 at the king's request, but he resigned and spent the civil war years at Lambeth Palace.[46] Charles later requested Juxon to attend him as chaplain at his execution. When the Bishopric of London was abolished during the interregnum, Juxon moved to Little Compton in Gloucester, where he remained until the restoration. Juxon was not troubled by the authorities during this time, for several reasons. Firstly, the new regime was not about to engage on an orgy of blood-letting on its former enemies. Unlike the aftermath of the French Revolution in the eighteenth century, there was no comparable 'reign of terror' directed against defeated royalists during the 1650s. Rebels and troublemakers were executed, of course, but the young republic was keen to demonstrate its gentleness. William Juxon was loyal to the church, but he was determined not to be cast as either rebel or troublemaker. Juxon thus survived the interregnum. At the restoration, he was elevated to Archbishop of Canterbury, but was in his late 70s and in declining health. He served as archbishop, however, until his death, aged 80, in 1663.[47] Juxon is commemorated in the city by Juxon House facing the 'new' St Paul's Cathedral, built after the old St Paul's was burnt down in 1666.[48]

Like much of the ancient and medieval city that stood in the 1640s, very little remains nowadays. The Great Fire of London in 1666 killed very few people but eighty percent of the city was destroyed. St Paul's Cathedral, the city churches and most of the halls of the city livery companies that stand today are post-fire, some of them rebuilt after the Blitz in the Second World War. The medieval Guildhall, the Tower of London, the remaining sections of the old Roman walls, and a handful of stone fragments of the Cheapside Cross in the Museum of London are virtually all that is left in the city of the buildings and structures of this period. However, we have the records and histories of the city livery companies and parliament. There is also a wealth of private journals, diaries, newsbooks. From these, this narrative history of the City of London and how it found itself involved in a civil war not necessarily of its own choice was constructed. In setting this narrative against the backdrop of wider issues of the history of the three kingdoms in the early seventeenth century, the author has attempted to anchor the story of London and the civil wars in a wider context.

This is, however, necessarily a limited survey and there are many more stories about London, before, during, and after the civil wars yet to be explored.

Endnotes

Chapter 1: James and Charles 1603–1640

1. Stephen Porter, *Lord Have Mercy Upon Us: London's Plague Years*, (Stroud, 2005), pp80, 83.
2. Allan I. Macinnes, 'The Multiple Kingdoms of Britain and Ireland', *A Companion to Stuart Britain*, Ed Barry Coward, (Oxford, 2009), p4.
3. http://www.historyofparliamentonline.org/research/parliaments/parliaments-1604-1629. Accessed 26 March 2017.
4. http://www.historyofparliamentonline.org/volume/1604-1629/survey/parliament-1604-1610#footnote9_ep3bjaa. Accessed 26 March 2017.
5. http://www.historyofparliamentonline.org/research/parliaments/parliaments-1604-1629 accessed 29 May 2017
6. Samuel Rawson Gardiner, *Dictionary of National Biography*, 1885-1900, Volume 29, p172.
7. Gardiner, *Dictionary of National Biography*, p180-181.
8. Gardiner, *Dictionary of National Biography*, p173.
9. *King James Authorised Bible*, Proverbs, Chapter 16, Verse 18.
10. Austin Woolrych, *Britain in Revolution 1625-1660*, (Oxford, 2002), p54.
11. Conrad Russell, 'The Nature of a Parliament in Early Stuart England', *Unrevolutionary England, 1603-1642*, (London, 1990), p9.
12. Woolrych, *Britain in Revolution*, p54.
13. Woolrych, *Britain in Revolution*, p53.
14. Woolrych, *Britain in Revolution*, p54.
15. Woolrych, *Britain in Revolution*, p55.
16. Woolrych, *Britain in Revolution*, p56.
17. http://www.historyofparliamentonline.org/volume/1604-1629/member/cromwell-oliver-1599-1658 accessed 29 May 2017
18. Woolrych, *Britain in Revolution*, p58.
19. *Commons Debates for 1629, critically edited and an introduction dealing with parliamentary sources for the early Stuarts*, (Ed), Wallace Notestein and Helen Relf, (Minneapolis, 1921), pp101-102.
20. *Commons Debates for 1629*, pp104-105.
21. Diane Purkiss, *The English Civil War: A People's History*, (London, 2007), p26, 28
22. Purkiss, *The English Civil War*, p85.
23. Samuel Rawson Gardiner, *History of England, Volume 9, from the Accession of James I to the Outbreak of the Civil War, 1603-1642*, Volume 9, 1639-1641, (London, 2005,) p214.
24. Porter, *Lord Have Mercy Upon Us*, pp148, 159.

25. Paul Slack, *The Impact of Plague in Tudor and Stuart London*, (London, 1985), p153.
26. Porter, *Lord Have Mercy Upon Us*, p154.
27. Porter, *Lord Have Mercy Upon Us*, p156.
28. Valerie Pearl, *London and the Puritan Revolution: National Government and City Politics, 1625-43*, London, 1961, p23.
29. Robert Ashton, *The City and the Court, 1603-1643*, (London, 1979), p164.
30. Ashton, *The City and the Court*, p164.
31. Pearl, *London and the Outbreak of the Puritan Revolution*, p24.
32. Pearl, *London and the Outbreak of the Puritan Revolution*, p24.
33. Ashton, *The City and the Court*, p164-5.
34. Pearl, *London and the Outbreak of the Puritan Revolution*, p32.
35. Pearl, *London and the Outbreak of the Puritan Revolution*, p32.
36. 'Municipal institutions', in *Analytical Index to the Series of Records Known as the Remembrancia 1579-1664*, ed. W H Overall and H C Overall (London, 1878), pp. 227-229. *British History Online* http://www.british-history.ac.uk/no-series/index-remembrancia/1579-1664/pp227-229 [accessed 19 March 2017].
37. Ashton, *The City and the Court*, p166.
38. Ashton, *The City and the Court*, p28
39. Ashton, *The City and the Court*, p30.
40. N.A.M. Rodger, *The Safeguard of the Sea: A Naval History of Britain, 660-1649*, (London, 2004), p393.
41. Woolrych, *Britain in Revolution*, p67.
42. Rodger, *The Safeguard of the Sea*, p393.
43. John Rushworth, 'Historical Collections: 1636', in *Historical Collections of Private Passages of State: Volume 2, 1629-38*(London, 1721), pp. 319-378. *British History Online* http://www.british-history.ac.uk/rushworth-papers/vol2/pp319-378 [accessed 6 April 2017].
44. Purkiss, *The English Civil War*, p23.

Chapter 2: The long, the short and the fractious parliaments

1. John Dummelow. *The Wax Chandlers: A Short History of the Worshipful Company of Wax Chandlers of London*, (London, 1973), p65.
2. EN Williams, 'Strafford, Thomas Wentworth, Earl of', *Dictionary of English and European History, 1485-1789*, (London, 1980), p419
3. Samuel Rawson Gardiner, 'Wentworth Thomas, 1593-1641', *Dictionary of National Biography 1885-1900*, Volume 60, p277.
4. Gardiner, 'Wentworth Thomas, 1593-1641', *Dictionary of National Biography*, p277.
5. Ian Gentles, *The English Revolution and the Wars in Three Kingdoms, 1638-1652*, (Harlow, 2007), p25.
6. Samuel Rawson Gardiner, *History of England, Volume 9*,, p108.
7. Gardiner, *History of England, Volume 9*,, p109.
8. Gardiner, *History of England, Volume 9*,, p112.

9. http://www.historyofparliamentonline.org/volume/1604-1629/member/strode-william-1594-1645 accessed 4 June 2017.

10. http://www.historyofparliamentonline.org/volume/1604-1629/member/holles-denzil-1598-1680 accessed 4 June 2017.

11. 'House of Commons Journal Volume 2: 17 April 1640', in *Journal of the House of Commons: Volume 2, 1640-1643* (London, 1802), pp. 4-6. *British History Online* http://www.british-history.ac.uk/commons-jrnl/vol2/pp4-6 [accessed 29 April 2017].

12. Gardiner, *History of England, Volume 9,*, p117.

13. 'House of Commons Journal Volume 2: 05 May 1640', in *Journal of the House of Commons: Volume 2, 1640-1643* (London, 1802), p. 19. *British History Online* http://www.british-history.ac.uk/commons-jrnl/vol2/p19a [accessed 29 April 2017].

14. Gardiner, *History of England, Volume 9,*, p118.

15. Gardiner, *History of England, Volume 9,*, p130.

16. Gardiner, *History of England, Volume 9,*, p133.

17. Gardiner, *History of England, Volume 9,*, p133.

18. Gardiner, *History of England, Volume 9,*, p141-142.

19. Gardiner, *History of England, Volume 9,*, p142-143.

20. Conrad Russell, 'The Nature of a Parliament in Early Stuart England', *Unrevolutionary England, 1603-1642*, (London, 1990), p2.

21. Russell, *Unrevolutionary England*, p2.

22. Russell, *Unrevolutionary England*, p4.

23. 'March 1642: Ordinance for settling the Militia of London agreed to.', in *Acts and Ordinances of the Interregnum, 1642-1660*, ed. C H Firth and R S Rait (London, 1911), pp. 5-6. *British History Online* http://www.british-history.ac.uk/no-series/acts-ordinances-interregnum/pp5-6 [accessed 27 May 2017].

24. 'March 1642: Ordinance for settling the Militia of London agreed to.', in *Acts and Ordinances of the Interregnum, 1642-1660*, ed. C H Firth and R S Rait (London, 1911), pp. 5-6. *British History Online* http://www.british-history.ac.uk/no-series/acts-ordinances-interregnum/pp5-6 [accessed 27 May 2017].

25. Barry Coward, *The Stuart Age: England 1603-1714*, (4th Edition, Harlow, 2012), p188.

26. Coward, *The Stuart Age*, p188.

27. 'May 1642: The Ordinance for raising Men for Ireland.', in *Acts and Ordinances of the Interregnum, 1642-1660*, ed. C H Firth and R S Rait (London, 1911), p. 6. *British History Online* http://www.british-history.ac.uk/no-series/acts-ordinances-interregnum/p6 [accessed 27 May 2017].

28. Woolrych, *Britain in Revolution*, pp221-222.

29. Coward, *The Stuart Age*, p190-91.

30. Coward, *The Stuart Age*, p190-91.

31. Rushworth and John, 'Historical Collections: Of the King's Commission of Array', in *Historical Collections of Private Passages of State: Volume 4, 1640-42* (London, 1721), pp. 655-688. *British History Online* http://www.british-history.ac.uk/rushworth-papers/vol4/pp655-688 [accessed 27 May 2017].

Chapter 3: Heart of the city

1. (Ed Ben Weinreb), *The London Encyclopaedia*, Third Edition, (London, 2008), pp511-512.
2. Simon Bradley and Nicholas Pevsner, *The Buildings of England: London 1, The City of London*, (London, 2002), p298-299,303-306.
3. C.P. Hill. *Who's Who in Stuart Britain*, Second Edition, (London, 1988), p239, 280.
4. Hill. *Who's Who in Stuart Britain*, pp280-283.
5. Peter Gaunt, *The Cromwellian Gazetteer: An Illustrated Guide to Britain in the Civil War and Commonwealth*, ((Stroud, 2000), p68.
6. Alexander Gordon, 'John Tillotson', *Dictionary of National Biography*, 1885-1900, Volume 56, pp293-298.
7. *The London Encyclopaedia*, p780.
8. *The London Encyclopaedia*, p600.
9. Samuel Rawson Gardiner, *History of the Commonwealth and Protectorate*, Volume 2, pp100-101.
10. Gardiner, *Commonwealth and Protectorate*, Volume 4, pp13-14.
11. Gardiner, *Commonwealth and Protectorate*, Volume 2, p201.
12. Gardiner, *Commonwealth and Protectorate*, Volume 4, pp15-117.
13. https://www.cityoflondon.gov.uk/things-to-do/green-spaces/management-of-our-green-spaces/Pages/default.aspx
14. C.R.N. Routh, *Who's Who in Tudor England*, (London, 1990), p204.
15. Hill. *Who's Who in Stuart Britain*, p128
16. Hill. *Who's Who in Stuart Britain*, pp68-69.
17. Hill. *Who's Who in Stuart Britain*, pp71-72.
18. Hill. *Who's Who in Stuart Britain*, p72.
19. Samuel Rawson Gardiner, *History of England, Volume 9,*, p341.
20. Barry Coward, *The Stuart Age*, p184.
21. Robert Ashton, 'The Role of the City in the Great Rebellion', *London and the Civil War*, (Ed. Stephen Porter), London, 1996, p.51.
22. Woolrych, *Britain in Revolution*, pp211-212.
23. Woolrych, *Britain in Revolution*, p212.
24. Woolrych, *Britain in Revolution*, p213.
25. 'Charles I, 1640: An Act for the preventing of inconveniencies happening by the long intermission of Parliaments.', in *Statutes of the Realm: Volume 5, 1628-80*, ed. John Raithby (s.l, 1819), pp. 54-57. *British History Online* http://www.british-history.ac.uk/statutes-realm/vol5/pp54-57 [accessed 17 March 2017].
26. http://www.parliament.uk/about/mps-and-lords/principal/black-rod/
27. John Adamson, *The Noble Revolt: The Overthrow of Charles I*, (London, 2007), p497.
28. Ian Roy, '"This Proud Unthankful City": A Cavalier View of London in the Civil War", *London and the Civil War*, p154.
29. Woolrych, *Britain in Revolution*, p213.
30. Woolrych, *Britain in Revolution*, p214.
31. Samuel Rawson Gardiner, *History of the Great Civil War 1642-1649*, Volume 1, (Adlestrop, 1987), p51.

32. Victor Smith and Peter Kelsey, 'The Lines of Communication', *London and the Civil War*, p118.

33. Alfred P Beaven, 'Chronological list of aldermen: 1601-1650', in *The Aldermen of the City of London Temp. Henry III - 1912*(London, 1908), pp. 47-75. *British History Online* http://www.british-history.ac.uk/no-series/london-aldermen/hen3-1912/pp47-75 [accessed 29 May 2017].

34. Ashton, *The City and the Court*, p206.

35. 'House of Lords Journal Volume 5: 12 August 1642', in *Journal of the House of Lords: Volume 5, 1642-1643* (London, 1767-1830), pp. 284-286. *British History Online* http://www.british-history.ac.uk/lords-jrnl/vol5/pp284-286 [accessed 18 March 2017].

36. 'House of Commons Journal Volume 6: 5 August 1651', in *Journal of the House of Commons: Volume 6, 1648-1651* (London, 1802), pp. 615-617. *British History Online* http://www.british-history.ac.uk/commons-jrnl/vol6/pp615-617 [accessed 18 March 2017].

37. Charlotte Fell Smith, 'Isaac Pennington', *Dictionary of National Biography*, 1885-1900, Volume 44, pp295-297.

38. Alfred P Beaven, 'Chronological list of aldermen: 1601-1650', in *The Aldermen of the City of London Temp. Henry III - 1912*(London, 1908), pp. 47-75. *British History Online* http://www.british-history.ac.uk/no-series/london-aldermen/hen3-1912/pp47-75 [accessed 29 May 2017].

39. 'December 1643: An Ordinance to disable any person within the City of London and Liberties thereof, to be of the Common-Council, or in any Office of trust within the said City, that shall not take the late solemn League and Covenant.' in *Acts and Ordinances of the Interregnum, 1642-1660*, ed. C H Firth and R S Rait (London, 1911), p. 359. *British History Online* http://www.british-history.ac.uk/no-series/acts-ordinances-interregnum/p359 [accessed 18 March 2017].

40. Alfred P Beaven, 'Notes on the aldermen, 1502-1700', in *The Aldermen of the City of London Temp. Henry III - 1912* (London, 1908), pp. 168-195. *British History Online* http://www.british-history.ac.uk/no-series/london-aldermen/hen3-1912/pp168-195 [accessed 29 May 2017].

41. Nicholas Pocock, 'Thomas Adams', *Dictionary of National Biography*, 1885-1900, Volume 2, p102.

42. Gordon Goodwin, 'John Gayer', *Dictionary of National Biography*, 1885-1900, p91-93

43. John Emberton, *Skippon's Brave Boys: The Origin, Development, and Civil War Service of London's Trained Bands*, (Buckingham, 1984), p53.

44. Gardiner, *History of the Great Civil War*, Volume 4, p46.

45. Gardiner, *History of the Great Civil War*, Volume 4, p98.

46. Gardiner, *History of the Great Civil War*, Volume 4, pp144-145.

47. Alfred P Beaven, 'Chronological list of aldermen: 1601-1650', in *The Aldermen of the City of London Temp. Henry III - 1912* (London, 1908), pp. 47-75. *British History Online* http://www.british-history.ac.uk/no-series/london-aldermen/hen3-1912/pp47-75 [accessed 31 May 2017].

48. Charles M. Clode, *London During the Great Rebellion: Being a Memoir of Sir Abraham Reynardsen KT*, (London, 1892), p5,

49. Charles Welch, 'Abraham Reynardsen', *Dictionary of National Biography*, 1885-1900, Volume 44, pp35-36.

50. Welch, 'Abraham Reynardsen', p35.

51. Robert Brenner, *Merchants and Revolution: Commercial Change, Political Conflict, and London's Overseas Traders, 1550-1653*, (London, 2003), p422

52. Mark Noble, *The lives of the English regicides: and other commissioners of the pretended High court of justice, appointed to sit in judgement upon their sovereign, King Charles the First, Volume 1*, (London, 1798), pp81-82.

53. Peter Gaunt, *The Cromwellian Gazetteer: An Illustrated Guide to Britain in the Civil War and Commonwealth*, (Stroud, 2000), pp65-66.

54. Michael Braddick, *God's Fury, England's Fire: A New History of the English Civil Wars*, (London, 2008), p493.

55. Gardiner, *Commonwealth and Protectorate*, Volume 4, pp45, 53.

56. Noble, *The Lives of the English Regicides*, pp81-82

57. Welch, 'Abraham Reynardsen', p35.

58. Gardiner, *History of the Great Civil War*, Volume 3, p146.

59. Gardiner, *History of the Great Civil War*, Volume 3, p138.

60. 'August 1642: Ordinance for raising Money in London.', in *Acts and Ordinances of the Interregnum, 1642-1660*, ed. C H Firth and R S Rait (London, 1911), pp. 24-25. *British History Online* http://www.british-history.ac.uk/no-series/acts-ordinances-interregnum/pp24-25 [accessed 8 February 2017].

61. 'August 1642: Ordinance for raising Money in London.'

62. 'August 1642: Ordinance for raising Money in London.'

63. Ian Gentles, *The English Revolution*, pp109-110.

64. *Calendar of The Proceedings of the Committee for Compounding &c, 1643-1660*, (Vol 1), (Ed) Mary Anne Everett Green, London, 1889, pp. v.

65. *Calendar of The Proceedings of the Committee for Compounding &c, 1643-1660*, (Vol 1), pp.vi.

66. Gardiner, *History of the Great Civil War*, Volume 3, p216.

67. 'October 1647: An Ordinance for disabling Delinquents to bear Office, or to have any voice in the election of any.', in *Acts and Ordinances of the Interregnum, 1642-1660*, ed. C H Firth and R S Rait (London, 1911), pp. 1023-1025. *British History Online*http://www.british-history.ac.uk/no-series/acts-ordinances-interregnum/pp1023-1025 [accessed 2 June 2017].

68. Gardiner, *History of the Great Civil War*, Volume 4, p270.

69. 'December 1648: An Ordinance concerning the Election of Common-council men and other Officers in the City of London.', in *Acts and Ordinances of the Interregnum, 1642-1660*, ed. C H Firth and R S Rait (London, 1911), p. 1253. *British History Online*http://www.british-history.ac.uk/no-series/acts-ordinances-interregnum/p1253 [accessed 9 April 2017].

Chapter 4: Mercers and other livery companies

1. Stephen Porter, *London and the Civil War*, (Basingstoke, 1996), p1.

2. *The London Encyclopaedia*, (Ed Ben Weinreb), Third Edition, (London, 2008), p175.

3. Ashton, *The City and the Court,* pp157-158.

4. Ashton, *The City and the Court,* p13.

5. Ashton, *The City and the Court,* p159.

6. Ashton, *The City and the Court,* p161.

7. *The London Encyclopaedia,* p180.

8. Brenner, *Merchants and Revolution,* p59.

9. Gardiner, *History of the Great Civil War,* Volume 3, p198.

10. https://www.thegoldsmiths.co.uk/company/history/history-of-the-company/ accessed 3 June 2017.

11. https://www.thegoldsmiths.co.uk/company/history/history-of-the-company/ accessed 13 May 2017.

12. https://www.thegoldsmiths.co.uk/company/history/history-hall/ accessed 13 May 2017.

13. https://www.thegoldsmiths.co.uk/company/history/history-of-the-company/ accessed 13 May 2017.

14. Lawrence H. Officer and Samuel H. Williamson, "Five Ways to Compute the Relative Value of a UK Pound Amount, 1270 to Present," MeasuringWorth, 2017. https://www.measuringworth.com/ppoweruk/ accessed 13 May 2017.

15. https://www.thegoldsmiths.co.uk/company/history/history-of-the-company/ accessed 13 May 2017.

16. http://www.armourershall.co.uk/armourers-and-brasiers-company accessed 12 May 2017.

17. Sydney Hewitt Pitt, *Some Notes on the History of the Worshipful Company of Armourers and Brasiers,* (Private Printing, 1930), p8-9.

18. Pitt, *Worshipful Company of Armourers and Brasiers,* p9.

19. Pitt, *Worshipful Company of Armourers and Brasiers,* pp18, 21.

20. Pitt, *Worshipful Company of Armourers and Brasiers,* p22.

21. 'House of Lords Journal Volume 5: 27 June 1642', in *Journal of the House of Lords: Volume 5, 1642-1643* (London, 1767-1830), pp. 163-167. *British History Online* http://www.british-history.ac.uk/lords-jrnl/vol5/pp163-167 [accessed 13 May 2017].

22. Pitt, *Worshipful Company of Armourers and Brasiers,* p37.

23. http://www.haberdashers.co.uk/content.php?p=company-history accessed 14 May 2017.

24. http://www.haberdashers.co.uk/content.php?p=hall-history accessed 14 May 2017.

25. http://www.haberdashers.co.uk/content.php?p=hall-history accessed 14 May 2017.

26. http://www.historyofparliamentonline.org/volume/1604-1629/member/howard-sir-edward-ii-1602-1675 accessed 14 May 2017.

27. http://www.historyofparliamentonline.org/volume/1604-1629/member/howard-sir-edward-ii-1602-1675 accessed 14 May 2017

28. Stephen Porter, 'The Economic and Social Impact', *London and the Civil War,* p178

29. 'House of Lords Journal Volume 6: 26 October 1643', in *Journal of the House of Lords: Volume 6, 1643* (London, 1767-1830), pp. 273-274. *British History Online* http://www.british-history.ac.uk/lords-jrnl/vol6/pp273-274 [accessed 3 June 2017].

30. Porter, 'The Economic and Social Impact', *London and the Civil War,* p187.

31. Porter, 'The Economic and Social Impact', *London and the Civil War*, p186.
32. Porter, 'The Economic and Social Impact', *London and the Civil War*, p194.
33. http://www.waxchandlers.org.uk/origins/index.php accessed 12 May 2017.
34. http://www.waxchandlers.org.uk/about-us/index.php accessed 12 May 2017.
35. http://www.waxchandlers.org.uk/the-hall/index.php accessed 12 May 2017.
36. John Watney, *An Account of the Mistery of Mercers of the City of London, otherwise known as known as the Mercers' Company*, (London, 1914), p56.
37. Watney, *An Account of the Mercers' Company*, p56-57.
38. Walter Thornbury, 'Cheapside: Northern tributaries (continued)', in *Old and New London: Volume 1* (London, 1878), pp. 374–383. *British History Online* http://www.british-history.ac.uk/old-new-london/vol1/pp374-383 [accessed 13 May 2017].
39. Leslie B. Prince, *The Farrier and His Craft: A History of the Worshipful Company of Farriers*, (London, 1980), p.3
40. http://www.loriner.co.uk/company-past-present/ accessed 13 May 1017.
41. http://www.wcf.org.uk/company.php accessed 13 May 2017.
42. Kingsley M. Oliver, *Hold Fast, Sit Sure: The History of the Worshipful Company of Saddlers of the City of London 1160-1960*, (Chichester, 1995), pp90-92.
43. Oliver, *Hold Fast, Sit Sure*, p92.
44. Oliver, *Hold Fast, Sit Sure*, p92.
45. Oliver, *Hold Fast, Sit Sure*, p92.
46. 'November 1642: Order Concerning Apprentices that list themselves for Soldiers.', in *Acts and Ordinances of the Interregnum, 1642-1660*, ed. C H Firth and R S Rait (London, 1911), p. 37. *British History Online* http://www.british-history.ac.uk/no-series/acts-ordinances-interregnum/p37 [accessed 19 May 2017].
47. Oliver, *Hold Fast, Sit Sure*, p93.
48. Oliver, *Hold Fast, Sit Sure*, p95-96.
49. Oliver, *Hold Fast, Sit Sure*, p95-96.
50. Walter Thornbury, 'Old Jewry', in *Old and New London: Volume 1* (London, 1878), pp. 425–435. *British History Online*http://www.british-history.ac.uk/old-new-london/vol1/pp425-435 [accessed 14 May 2017].
51. Walter Thornbury, 'Old Jewry', in *Old and New London: Volume 1* (London, 1878), pp. 425–435. *British History Online*http://www.british-history.ac.uk/old-new-london/vol1/pp425-435 [accessed 14 May 2017].
52. 'Industries: Tobacco', in *A History of the County of Middlesex: Volume 2, General; Ashford, East Bedfont With Hatton, Feltham, Hampton With Hampton Wick, Hanworth, Laleham, Littleton*, ed. William Page (London, 1911), p. 179. *British History Online*http://www.british-history.ac.uk/vch/middx/vol2/p179 [accessed 13 May 2017].
53. http://www.tobaccolivery.org/the-company.html#our-history accessed 12 May 2017.
54. http://www.cutlerslondon.co.uk/company/history/accesed 12 May 2017.
55. http://www.cutlerslondon.co.uk/company/history/ accessed 12 May 2017.
56. http://www.cutlerslondon.co.uk/company/history/ accessed 12 May 2017.
57. http://www.cutlerslondon.co.uk/hall/ accessed 12 May 2017.

58. Charles Welch, *History of the Cutlers' Company of London, Volume II, From 1500 to Modern Times*, (Private Printing, 1923), p89.

59. Welch, *History of the Cutlers' Company of London, Volume II*, p163.

60. 'July 1643: An Ordinance for the speedy Rising and Levying of Moneys, set by way of Charge or new Impost, on the several Commodities mentioned in the Schedule hereunto annexed; As well for the better securing of Trade, as for the maintenance of the Forces raised for the Defence of the King and Parliament, both by Sea and Land, as for and towards the Payment of the Debts of the Commonwealth, for which the Publique Faith is, or shall be given.', in *Acts and Ordinances of the Interregnum, 1642-1660*, ed. C H Firth and R S Rait (London, 1911), pp. 202-214. *British History Online* http://www.british-history.ac.uk/no-series/acts-ordinances-interregnum/pp202-214 [accessed 15 May 2017].

61. 'July 1643: An Ordinance for the speedy Rising and Levying of Moneys, set by way of Charge or new Impost, on the several Commodities mentioned in the Schedule hereunto annexed; As well for the better securing of Trade, as for the maintenance of the Forces raised for the Defence of the King and Parliament, both by Sea and Land, as for and towards the Payment of the Debts of the Commonwealth, for which the Publique Faith is, or shall be given.', in *Acts and Ordinances of the Interregnum, 1642-1660*, ed. C H Firth and R S Rait (London, 1911), pp. 202-214. *British History Online* http://www.british-history.ac.uk/no-series/acts-ordinances-interregnum/pp202-214 [accessed 15 May 2017].

62. 'July 1643: An Ordinance for the speedy Rising and Leavying of Moneys, set by way of Charge or new Impost, on the several Commodities mentioned in the Schedule hereunto annexed; Aswell for the better securing of Trade, as for the maintenance of the Forces raised for the Defence of the King and Parliament, both by Sea and Land, as for and towards the Payment of the Debts of the Commonwealth, for which the Publique Faith is, or shall be given.', in *Acts and Ordinances of the Interregnum, 1642-1660*, ed. C H Firth and R S Rait (London, 1911), pp. 202-214. *British History Online* http://www.british-history.ac.uk/no-series/acts-ordinances-interregnum/pp202-214 [accessed 15 May 2017].

63. http://www.historyofparliamentonline.org/volume/1660-1690/member/langham-john-1584-1671 accessed 15 May 2017.

Chapter 5: Religious strife

1. *The London Encyclopaedia*, p154.

2. *The London Encyclopaedia*, p808.

3. Gardiner, *History of the Great Civil War*, Volume 1, p132.

4. 'House of Commons Journal Volume 3: 24 April 1643', in *Journal of the House of Commons: Volume 3, 1643-1644* (London, 1802), pp. 57-58. *British History Online* http://www.british-history.ac.uk/commons-jrnl/vol3/pp57-58 [accessed 14 April 2017].

5. Julie Spraggon. *Puritan Iconoclasm during the English Civil War*, (Woodbridge, 2003), p85.

6. Gardiner, *History of the Great Civil War*, Volume 1, p132.

7. Spraggon. *Puritan Iconoclasm*, p62-63.

8. Spraggon. *Puritan Iconoclasm*, p257.

9. 'Cheapside Cross', in *Analytical Index to the Series of Records Known as the Remembrancia 1579-1664*, ed. W H Overall and H C Overall (London, 1878), pp. 65-66. *British History Online* http://www.british-history.ac.uk/no-series/index-remembrancia/1579-1664/pp65-66 (Footnote 2) [accessed 14 April 2017].

10. Spraggon. *Puritan Iconoclasm*, p159.

11. 'May 1644: An Ordinance for the further demolishing of Monuments of Idolatry and Superstition.', in *Acts and Ordinances of the Interregnum, 1642-1660*, ed. C H Firth and R S Rait (London, 1911), pp. 425-426. *British History Online* http://www.british-history.ac.uk/no-series/acts-ordinances-interregnum/pp425-426 [accessed 14 April 2017].

12. *The London Encyclopaedia*, p809.

13. *The London Encyclopaedia*, p809.

14. 'Paul's, St, cathedral of', in *Analytical Index to the Series of Records Known as the Remembrancia 1579-1664*, ed. W H Overall and H C Overall (London, 1878), pp. 322-329. *British History Online* http://www.british-history.ac.uk/no-series/index-remembrancia/1579-1664/pp322-329 [accessed 14 April 2017].

15. *The London Encyclopaedia*, p809.

16. *The London Encyclopaedia*, p859, 1006-7.

17. Gardiner, *History of the Great Civil War*, Volume 1, p304.

18. Spraggon. *Puritan Iconoclasm*, p262.

19. Spraggon. *Puritan Iconoclasm*, p263.

20. Spraggon. *Puritan Iconoclasm*, p263.

21. Gordon Goodwin, 'Henry Mildmay', *Dictionary of National Biography, 1885-1900*, Volume 37, pp372-374

22. John Adamson, *The Noble Revolt*, p255.

23. http://www.historyofparliamentonline.org/volume/1604-1629/member/mildmay-sir-henry-1594-1668 [accessed 25 April 2017]

24. Gardiner, *History of the Great Civil War*, Volume 3, p199.

25. 'House of Commons Journal Volume 3: 22 March 1643', in *Journal of the House of Commons: Volume 3, 1643-1644* (London, 1802), pp. 12-14. *British History Online* http://www.british-history.ac.uk/commons-jrnl/vol3/pp12-14 [accessed 17 April 2017].

26. Walter Thornbury, 'Bartholomew Lane and Lombard Street', in *Old and New London: Volume 1* (London, 1878), pp. 522-530. *British History Online* http://www.british-history.ac.uk/old-new-london/vol1/pp522-530 [accessed 17 April 2017].

27. Gardiner, *History of the Great Civil War*, Volume 3, p199.

28. William MC Murray (Ed), *The Records of Two City Parishes: A Collection of Documents Illustrative of the History of St Anne and Agnes, Aldersgate and St John Zachery London*, (London, 1925), p283.

29. John Rushworth, 'Historical Collections: The trial of William Laud', in *Historical Collections of Private Passages of State: Volume 3, 1639-40* (London, 1721), pp. 1365-1381. *British History Online* http://www.british-history.ac.uk/rushworth-papers/vol3/pp1365-1381 [accessed 17 April 2017].

30. Gardiner, *History of England, Volume 9,*, Volume 9, p296.
31. http://www.constitution.org/eng/conpur043.htm [Accessed 25 April 2017]
32. Rushworth and John, 'Historical Collections: December 1641', in *Historical Collections of Private Passages of State: Volume 4, 1640-42* (London, 1721), pp. 436-471. *British History Online* http://www.british-history.ac.uk/rushworth-papers/vol4/pp436-471 [accessed 25 April 2017].
33. Woolrych, *Britain in Revolution*, p182, 295.
34. Rushworth and John, 'Historical Collections: December 1641', in *Historical Collections of Private Passages of State: Volume 4, 1640-42* (London, 1721), pp. 436-471. *British History Online* http://www.british-history.ac.uk/rushworth-papers/vol4/pp436-471 [accessed 25 April 2017].
35. Gardiner, *History of the Great Civil War*, Volume 1, p246-7.
36. Gardiner, *History of the Great Civil War*, Volume 2, p99-100.
37. Woolrych, *Britain in Revolution*, p295.
38. 'January 1645: Ordinance for the Attainder of the Archbishop of Canterbury.', in *Acts and Ordinances of the Interregnum, 1642-1660*, ed. C H Firth and R S Rait (London, 1911), p. 608. *British History Online* http://www.british-history.ac.uk/no-series/acts-ordinances-interregnum/p608 [accessed 17 April 2017].
39. Gardiner, *History of the Great Civil War*, Volume 1, pp99-100
40. Ian Gentles, *The English Revolution and the Wars in Three Kingdoms*, ((Harlow, 2007), pp247.
41. Gardiner, *History of the Great Civil War*, Volume 2, p190.
42. Spraggon. *Puritan Iconoclasm*, p262.
43. Gentles, *The English Revolution*, pp7-8.
44. Gardiner, *History of the Great Civil War*, Volume 2, p101.
45. Spraggon. *Puritan Iconoclasm*, p144.
46. Spraggon. *Puritan Iconoclasm*, p144.
47. Spraggon. *Puritan Iconoclasm*, p144, footnote 1 and 2.
48. Spraggon. *Puritan Iconoclasm*, p162.
49. Spraggon. *Puritan Iconoclasm*, p173.
50. Alexander Gordon. 'John Goodwin', *Dictionary of National Biography, 1885-1900*, Volume 22, p145.
51. Gordon. 'John Goodwin', p146.
52. Purkiss, *The English Civil War*, p566
53. 'Charles II, 1660: An Act of Free and General Pardon Indemnity and Oblivion.', in *Statutes of the Realm: Volume 5, 1628-80*, ed. John Raithby (s.l, 1819), pp. 226-234. *British History Online* http://www.british-history.ac.uk/statutes-realm/vol5/pp226-234 [accessed 25 April 2017].
54. Ann Hughes, 'Religion 1640-1660', *A Companion to Stuart Britain*. Martin Bennet, *The English Civil War: A Historical Companion*, (Stroud, 2000), p92-93.
55. Hughes, 'Religion 1640-1660', p350.
56. Hughes, 'Religion 1640-1660', p364-365.
57. Diane Purkiss, *The English Civil War*, p48.
58. Gerald Aylmer, *Rebellion or Revolution: England 1640-1660*, (Oxford, 1987)
59. Gordon. 'John Goodwin', p147.

60. Bennet, *The English Civil War*, p232.

61. Woolrych, *Britain in Revolution*, p789

62. Alexander Balloch Grosart, 'Richard Baxter', *Dictionary of National Biography, 1885-1900*, Volume 03, p433.

63. Grosart, 'Richard Baxter', pp432-433.

64. Grosart, 'Richard Baxter', p434.

Chapter 6: Publish what you like?

1. https://stationers.org/about.html

2. 'Second Parliament of Great Britain: Second session - begins 13/11/1709', in *The History and Proceedings of the House of Commons: Volume 4, 1706-1713* (London, 1742), pp. 135-168. *British History Online* http://www.british-history.ac.uk/commons-hist-proceedings/vol4/pp135-168 [accessed 26 May 2017].

3. Ian Atherton, 'The Press and Popular Political Opinion', *A Companion to Stuart Britain*, p98.

4. Christiane J. Hessler, '*Ne supra trepipam suitor*', *Fifteenth Century Studies*, 33 (2008), 133-150.

5. Cyprian Blagden, *The Stationers' Company: A History 1403-1959*, London, 1960, p110.

6. C.H. Timperley, *Encyclopaedia of Literary and Typographical Anecdote, (1842),* p484

7. Blagden, *The Stationers Company*, p114.

8. Woolrych, *Britain in Revolution*, p184

9. Blagden, *The Stationers Company*, p130.

10. Atherton, 'The Press and Popular Political Opinion', *A Companion to Stuart Britain*, p93-94.

11.

12. Eleanor Chance, Christina Colvin, Janet Cooper, C J Day, T G Hassall, Mary Jessup and Nesta Selwyn, 'Early Modern Oxford', in *A History of the County of Oxford: Volume 4, the City of Oxford*, ed. Alan Crossley and C R Elrington (London, 1979), pp. 74-180. *British History Online* http://www.british-history.ac.uk/vch/oxon/vol4/pp74-180 [accessed 3 June 2017].

13. Thomas N. Corns, 'Literature and History', *A Companion to Stuart Britain*, p179.

14. Purkiss, *The English Civil War*, p282, p.285

15. *Mercurius Aulicus: A Diurnall Communicating the Intelligence and Affaires of the Court to the Rest of the Kingdom*, (Ed Frederick John Varley), (Oxford, 1948), v.

16. Thomas Seccombe, 'Bruno Ryves', *Dictionary of National Biography, 1885-1900*, Volume 50, p71.

17. John Walter, *Understanding Popular Violence in the English Revolution: the Colchester Plunderers*, (Cambridge/New York, 1999)

18. Thomas Seccombe, 'Bruno Ryves', *Dictionary of National Biography*, Volume 50, p71.

19. Edward Irving Carlyle, 'Nehemiah Wallington', *Dictionary of National Biography*, Volume 59, p138-9.

20. Charles Harding Firth, 'William Prynne', *Dictionary of National Biography*, Volume 46, p432-433

21. Alexander Balloch Grosart, 'John Bastwick', *Dictionary of National Biography*, Volume 3, p389-390

22. Grosart, 'John Bastwick', *Dictionary of National Biography*, Volume 3, p390

23. Grosart, 'John Bastwick', *Dictionary of National Biography*, Volume 3, p390

24. Charles Harding Firth, 'John Lilburne', *Dictionary of National Biography*, Volume 33, p243

25. John Rushworth, 'Historical Collections: 1637 (3 of 5)', in *Historical Collections of Private Passages of State: Volume 2, 1629-38*(London, 1721), pp. 461-481. *British History Online* http://www.british-history.ac.uk/rushworth-papers/vol2/pp461-481 [accessed 23 May 2017].

26. John Rushworth, 'Historical Collections: 1637 (3 of 5)', in *Historical Collections of Private Passages of State: Volume 2, 1629-38*(London, 1721), pp. 461-481. *British History Online* http://www.british-history.ac.uk/rushworth-papers/vol2/pp461-481 [accessed 23 May 2017].

27. Charles Harding Firth, 'John Lilburne', *Dictionary of National Biography*, Volume 33, p243

28. 'House of Commons Journal Volume 2: 04 May 1641', in *Journal of the House of Commons: Volume 2, 1640-1643* (London, 1802), pp. 133-134. *British History Online* http://www.british-history.ac.uk/commons-jrnl/vol2/pp133-134 [accessed 23 May 2017].

29. Firth, 'John Lilburne', p244.

30. Firth, 'John Lilburne', p244.

31. Firth, 'John Lilburne', p246.

32. 'June 1643: An Ordinance for the Regulating of Printing.', in *Acts and Ordinances of the Interregnum, 1642-1660*, ed. C H Firth and R S Rait (London, 1911), pp. 184-186. *British History Online* http://www.british-history.ac.uk/no-series/acts-ordinances-interregnum/pp184-186 [accessed 21 May 2017].

33. Charles Harding Firth, 'William Prynne, *Dictionary of National Biography, 1885-1900*, Volume 46, p433.

34. Purkiss, The English Civil War, p285

35. 'September 1647: An Ordinance against unlicensed or scandalous Pamphlets, and for the better Regulating of Printing.', in *Acts and Ordinances of the Interregnum, 1642-1660*, ed. C H Firth and R S Rait (London, 1911), pp. 1021-1023. *British History Online* http://www.british-history.ac.uk/no-series/acts-ordinances-interregnum/pp1021-1023 [accessed 22 May 2017].

36. 'September 1647: An Ordinance against unlicensed or scandalous Pamphlets, and for the better Regulating of Printing.', in *Acts and Ordinances of the Interregnum, 1642-1660*, ed. C H Firth and R S Rait (London, 1911), pp. 1021-1023. *British History Online* http://www.british-history.ac.uk/no-series/acts-ordinances-interregnum/pp1021-1023 [accessed 22 May 2017].

37. 'September 1649: An Act against Unlicensed and Scandalous Books and Pamphlets, and for better regulating of Printing.', in *Acts and Ordinances of the Interregnum, 1642-1660*, ed. C H Firth and R S Rait (London, 1911), pp.

245-254. *British History Online* http://www.british-history.ac.uk/no-series/acts-ordinances-interregnum/pp245-254 [accessed 22 May 2017].

38. Blagden, *The Stationer's Company*, p146.
39. 'September 1649: An Act against Unlicensed and Scandalous Books and Pamphlets, and for better regulating of Printing.', in *Acts and Ordinances of the Interregnum, 1642-1660*, ed. C H Firth and R S Rait (London, 1911), pp. 245-254. *British History Online* http://www.british-history.ac.uk/no-series/acts-ordinances-interregnum/pp245-254 [accessed 22 May 2017].
40. Blagden, *The Stationer's Company*, p147.
41. Blagden, *The Stationer's Company*, p147-8.
42. John Rees. *The Leveller Revolution: Radical Political Organisation in England, 1640-1650*, (London/New York, 2016), p43.
43. *The Agreement of the People, as presented to the Council of the Army*, 28 October 1647, http://www.constitution.org/eng/conpur074.htm. Accessed 25 May 2017.
44. Firth, 'John Lilburne', *Dictionary of National Biography*, p246
45. Bennet, *The English Civil War*, pp64–65.
46. Hill, *Who's Who in Stuart Britain*, p96.
47. Gardiner, *History of the Great Civil War*, Volume 3, p.380
48. Rees. *The Leveller Revolution*, p293-294.
49. Rees. *The Leveller Revolution*, p294.
50. Rees. *The Leveller Revolution*, p294.
51. Gardiner, *History of the Great Civil War*, Volume 3, p.380.
52. Gentles, 'Political Funerals during the English Revolution', *London and the Civil War*, p205.
53. Woolrych, *Britain in Revolution*, p445. Purkiss, *The English Civil War*, pp499-500.
54. Gentles, 'Political Funerals during the English Revolution', *London and the Civil War*, p225.

Chapter 7: London's brave boys: the trained bands and the defence of London

1. Wilfred Emberton, *Skippon's Brave Boys: The Origins, Development and Civil War Service of London's Trained Bands*, (Buckingham, 1984), p29.
2. Emberton, *Skippon's Brave Boys*, p29.
3. Lucy Hutchinson, *Memoirs of the Life of Colonel Hutchinson: Charles I's Puritan Nemesis*, (Ed. N. H. Keeble), (London, 2000), p84.
4. Emberton, *Skippon's Brave Boys*, p30.
5. Richard Venn is not known to be related to regicide John Venn.
6. Emberton, *Skippon's Brave Boys*, p30.
7. Emberton, *Skippon's Brave Boys*, p30. Lawson Nagel, 'A Great Bouncing at Every Man's Door: The Struggle for the London Militia in 1642', *London and the Civil War*, p.65.
8. http://www.historyofparliamentonline.org/volume/1604-1629/member/lowe-sir-thomas-1546-1623
9. http://www.historyofparliamentonline.org/volume/1604-1629/member/bond-martin-1558-1643

10. Emberton, *Skippon's Brave Boys*, p30.
11. Charles M. Clode, *London during the Great Rebellion, being a Memoir of Abraham Richardson, Sheriff and Master of the Merchant Taylor's Company, 1640-41,* (London, 1892), p17.
12. 'April 1643: An Ordinance that the Committee for the Militia of London, shall have full power and authority to raise new Regiments of Volunteers, as well within the said City and Liberties, as without.', in *Acts and Ordinances of the Interregnum, 1642-1660,* ed. C H Firth and R S Rait (London, 1911), pp. 130-131. *British History Online* http://www.british-history.ac.uk/no-series/acts-ordinances-interregnum/pp130-131 [accessed 10 March 2017].
13. Emberton, *Skippon's Brave Boys*, p32.
14. Emberton, *Skippon's Brave Boys*, p32.
15. Edward, Earl Clarendon. *The History of the Rebellion and Civil Wars in England begun the in the year 1641,* (Ed, W. Dunn Macray), (Oxford, 1888), Volume 1, p509.
16. Emberton, *Skippon's Brave Boys*, p39
17. I. Opie and P. Opie, *The Oxford Dictionary of Nursery Rhymes*, Second Edition (Oxford, 1997), p 447.
18. John Noorthouck, 'Book 1, Ch. 12: The Civil War, to the execution of the King', in *A New History of London Including Westminster and Southwark* (London, 1773), pp. 175-195. *British History Online* http://www.british-history.ac.uk/no-series/new-history-london/pp175-195 [accessed 13 March 2017].
19. John Noorthouck, 'Book 1, Ch. 12: The Civil War, to the execution of the King', in *A New History of London Including Westminster and Southwark* (London, 1773), pp. 175-195. *British History Online* http://www.british-history.ac.uk/no-series/new-history-london/pp175-195 [accessed 10 March 2017].
20. Norman Brett-James, *The Growth of Stuart London*, (London, 1935), p269.
21. Brett-James, *The Growth of Stuart London*, p269.
22. Calendar of State Papers, Venetian, 1642/43, 28 October-7
23. Victor Smith and Peter Kelsey, 'The Lines of Communication: The Civil War Defences of London', *London and the Civil War*, p121.
24. 'September 1647: Ordinance to slight the Works about London.', in *Acts and Ordinances of the Interregnum, 1642-1660,* ed. C H Firth and R S Rait (London, 1911), p. 1008. *British History Online* http://www.british-history.ac.uk/no-series/acts-ordinances-interregnum/p1008 [accessed 10 March 2017].
25. Victor Smith and Peter Kelsey, 'The Lines of Communication: The Civil War Defences of London', *London and the Civil War*, p144.
26. Smith and Kelsey, 'The Lines of Communication: The Civil War Defences of London', p145.
27. 'August 1643: An Ordinance of the Lords and Commons in Parliament assembled, concerning Forces to be sent, by the Committee of the Militia of the City of London, for the Relief of Gloucester.', in *Acts and Ordinances of the Interregnum, 1642-1660,* ed. C H Firth and R S Rait (London, 1911), pp. 260-261. *British History Online* http://www.british-history.ac.uk/no-series/acts-ordinances-interregnum/pp260-261 [accessed 10 March 2017].

28. John Noorthouck, 'Book 1, Ch. 12: The Civil War, to the execution of the King', in *A New History of London Including Westminster and Southwark* (London, 1773), pp. 175-195. *British History Online* http://www.british-history.ac.uk/no-series/new-history-london/pp175-195 [accessed 12 March 2017].

29. Emberton, *Skippon's Brave Boys*, p73.

30. Emberton, *Skippon's Brave Boys*, p81.

31. 'House of Lords Journal Volume 6: 5 August 1643', in *Journal of the House of Lords: Volume 6, 1643* (London, 1767-1830), pp. 171-172. *British History Online* http://www.british-history.ac.uk/lords-jrnl/vol6/pp171-172   [accessed   12 March 2017].

32. 'House of Commons Journal Volume 3: 7 August 1643', in *Journal of the House of Commons: Volume 3, 1643-1644* (London, 1802), pp. 196-198. *British History Online*   http://www.british-history.ac.uk/commons-jrnl/vol3/pp196-198 [accessed 12 March 2017].

33. Clode, *London during the Great Rebellion*, p26.

34. G.E. Aylmer, *Rebellion or Revolution?*, p55.

35. 'House of Commons Journal Volume 3: 7 August 1643', in *Journal of the House of Commons: Volume 3, 1643-1644* (London, 1802), pp. 196-198.

36. 'House of Commons Journal Volume 3: 7 August 1643', in *Journal of the House of Commons: Volume 3, 1643-1644* (London, 1802), pp. 196-198.

37. John Rushworth, 'Historical Collections: The Treaty of Oxford', in *Historical Collections of Private Passages of State: Volume 5, 1642-45* (London, 1721), pp. 164-263. *British History Online* http://www.british-history.ac.uk/rushworth-papers/vol5/pp164-263 [accessed 13 March 2017].

38. http://bcw-project.org/church-and-state/first-civil-war/nineteen-propositions. Accessed under Creative Commons Licence 13 March 2017.

39. Stephen Porter and Simon Maish, *The Battle for London*, (Stroud, 2010), p95-96.

40. 'December 1643: An Ordinance to enable the Militia of London, to send out Forces under Major General Browne.', in *Acts and Ordinances of the Interregnum, 1642-1660*, ed. C H Firth and R S Rait (London, 1911), pp. 359-360. *British History Online* http://www.british-history.ac.uk/no-series/acts-ordinances-interregnum/pp359-360 [accessed 10 March 2017].

41. Emberton, *Skippon's Brave Boys*, p101.

42 John Rushworth, 'Historical Collections: Essex's and Waller's armies, to June 1644', in *Historical Collections of Private Passages of State: Volume 5, 1642-45* (London, 1721), pp. 653-677. *British History Online* http://www.british-history.ac.uk/rushworth-papers/vol5/pp653-677 [accessed 7 June 2017].

43. Emberton, *Skippon's Brave Boys*, p108.

44. John Rushworth, 'Historical Collections: Essex's and Waller's armies, to June 1644', in *Historical Collections of Private Passages of State: Volume 5, 1642-45* (London, 1721), pp. 653-677. *British History Online* http://www.british-history.ac.uk/rushworth-papers/vol5/pp653-677 [accessed 7 June 2017].

45. Gerald Aylmer, *Rebellion or Revolution*, p58.

46. Purkiss, *The English Civil War*, p365.

47. Purkiss, *The English Civil War*, pp420-421.

48. Emberton, *Skippon's Brave Boys*, p119.
49. Gardiner, History of the Civil War, Volume 2, p5.

Chapter 8: To the winner the spoils: some later lives of stakeholders

1. John Noorthouck, 'Book 1, Ch. 13: To the Restoration', in *A New History of London Including Westminster and Southwark* (London, 1773), pp. 195-210. *British History Online* http://www.british-history.ac.uk/no-series/new-history-london/pp195-210 [accessed 4 June 2017].
2. Barry Coward, *The Cromwellian Protectorate*, (Manchester, 2002), pp8
3. 'December 1653: The Government of the Commonwealth of England, Scotland and Ireland, and the Dominions thereunto belonging.', in *Acts and Ordinances of the Interregnum, 1642-1660*, ed. C H Firth and R S Rait (London, 1911), pp. 813-822. *British History Online* http://www.british-history.ac.uk/no-series/acts-ordinances-interregnum/pp813-822 [accessed 4 June 2017].
4. Coward, *The Cromwellian Protectorate*, pp169-170.
5. Gardiner, *History of the Great Civil War*, Volume 4, p207.
6. Coward, *The Cromwellian Protectorate*, pp177-178
7. 'June 1654: An Ordinance for the Regulation of Hackney-Coachmen in London and the places adjacent.', in *Acts and Ordinances of the Interregnum, 1642-1660*, ed. C H Firth and R S Rait (London, 1911), pp. 922-924. *British History Online*http://www.british-history.ac.uk/no-series/acts-ordinances-interregnum/pp922-924 [accessed 4 June 2017].
8. Coward, *The Cromwellian Protectorate*, p89.
9. Coward, *The Cromwellian Protectorate*, p102.
10. Coward, *The Cromwellian Protectorate*, p103.
11. Coward, *The Cromwellian Protectorate*, p190.
12. Coward, *The Cromwellian Protectorate*, p112.
13. Samuel Rawson Gardiner, 'John Pym', *Dictionary of National Biography*, 1885-1900, Volume 47, pp82-83.
14. Gardiner, 'John Pym', *Dictionary of National Biography*, p83.
15. Charles Harding Firth, 'John Hampden', *Dictionary of National Biography*, p261.
16. Firth, 'William Strode', *Dictionary of National Biography*, p61
17. Firth, 'Denzil Holles', *Dictionary of National Biography*, p264-265.
18. 'Arthur Haselrig', *Encyclopedia Britannica*, 1911, p407
19. Peter Reese, *The Life of General George Monck: For King and Cromwell*, (Barnsley, 2008), pp19, 30.
20. Reese, *The Life of General George Monck*, p49.
21. Reese, *The Life of General George Monck*, pp65-7, 113-114.
22. Reese, *The Life of General George Monck*, p151.
23. Reese, *The Life of General George Monck*, pp166, 169-170.
24. Reese, *The Life of General George Monck*, p182.
25. Gardiner, *History of the Great Civil War*, Volume 4, p203.
26. Gardiner, *History of the Great Civil War*, Volume 4, p208.

27. Andrew Hopper, *'Black Tom': Sir Thomas Fairfax and the English Revolution*, (Manchester, 2007), p124.
28. Gardiner, *Commonwealth and Protectorate*, Volume 1, p5.
29. Gardiner, *Commonwealth and Protectorate*, Volume 1, p261
30. Gardiner, *Commonwealth and Protectorate*, Volume 3, p340
31. 'House of Commons Journal Volume 7: 5 August 1659', in *Journal of the House of Commons: Volume 7, 1651-1660* (London, 1802), pp. 747-749. *British History Online* http://www.british-history.ac.uk/commons-jrnl/vol7/pp747-749 [accessed 7 June 2017].
32. Firth, 'Philip Skippon', *Dictionary of National Biography*, pp255-256.
33. 'House of Commons Journal Volume 7: 16 November 1654', in *Journal of the House of Commons: Volume 7, 1651-1660*(London, 1802), pp. 385-386. *British History Online* http://www.british-history.ac.uk/commons-jrnl/vol7/pp385-386 [accessed 7 June 2017].
34. Hill, *Who's Who in Stuart Britain*, p95.
35. Hill, *Who's Who in Stuart Britain*, p95.
36. Purkiss, *The English Civil War*, p548
37. Gardiner, *Commonwealth and Protectorate*, Volume 1, p35
38. Hill, *Who's Who in Stuart Britain*, pp158-159.
39. EN Williams, *Dictionary of English and European History, 1485-1789*, (London, 1980), p94.
40. RC Richardson, *The Debate on the English Revolution*, Third Edition, (Manchester, 1998), p40.
41. Williams, *Dictionary of English and European History*, p95.
42. Hill, *Who's Who in Stuart Britain*, pp121-123.
43. Hill, *Who's Who in Stuart Britain*, p183.
44. Hill, *Who's Who in Stuart Britain*, p183.
45. Hill, *Who's Who in Stuart Britain*, pp184-185.
46. Hill, *Who's Who in Stuart Britain*, p81.
47. Hill, *Who's Who in Stuart Britain*, p81.
48. Bradley and Pevsner, *The Buildings of England*, p595.

Index